T0314766

CHILDREN OF POVERTY

Studies on the Effects of Single Parenthood, the Feminization of Poverty, and Homelessness

edited by

STUART BRUCHEY
Allan Nevins Professor Emeritus
Columbia University

TRANSITIONAL PROGRAMS FOR HOMELESS WOMEN WITH CHILDREN

EDUCATION, EMPLOYMENT TRAINING, AND SUPPORT SERVICES

JUDY KAY FLOHR

Routledge
Taylor & Francis Group
New York   London

First published by Garland Publishing, Inc.

This edition published 2011 by Routledge:

Routledge
Taylor & Francis Group
711 Third Avenue
New York, NY 10017

Routledge
Taylor & Francis Group
2 Park Square, Milton Park
Abingdon, Oxon OX14 4RN

Library of Congress Cataloging-in-Publication Data

Flohr, Judy K., 1954–
    Transitional programs for homeless women with children :
education, employment training, and support services / Judy K.
Flohr.
        p.   cm. — (Children of poverty)
    Includes bibliographical references and index.
    ISBN 0-8153-3316-1 (alk. paper)
    1. Homeless women—Services for—United States. 2. Single
mothers—Services for—United States. 3. Family services—United
States. I. Title. II. Series.
HV4505.F59 1998
362.83'086'942—dc21

                                                    98-46216

For all Homeless Women and their Families

Contents

TABLES   xi
ACKNOWLEDGMENTS   xv

1. INTRODUCTION   3
   Importance of the Study   3
   Background   4
   Purpose of the Study   9
   Research Questions   9
   Significance of the Study   10

2. LITERATURE REVIEW   11
   Definition of Homelessness   11
   Numbers of Homeless   12
   Characteristics of the Homeless   13
   The Causes of Homelessness   15
   Homeless Women with Children   17
      Historical Overview   17
      Economic and Social Factors   19
      Profile of Homeless Women with Children   20
   Profile of Emergency and Transitional Shelters/Housing   23
   Education and Employment Training   26
      Employment   26
      Education and Job Training   28
   Education and Job Training Programs   29
      Manpower Training Programs   30
      Job Training Partnership Act (JTPA)   31
      Stewart B. McKinney Homelessness Assistance Act   33

Adult Education for the Homeless (AHE) Program 34
Job Training for the Homeless Demonstration
Program (JTHDP) 35
Program Areas and Components 38
Summary 40

3. RESEARCH METHODS 43
Introduction 43
Population 44
Research Design 45
Analysis of Data 47
Limitations of the Study 49
Summary 49

4. PRESENTATION AND INTERPRETATION OF DATA 51
Research Methods 51
Goal 1: Identification, Characterization, and Analysis of
Current Transitional Programs for Homeless
Women With Children 52
Question 1: What are the profiles of the transitional
programs? 53
Question 2: What are the profiles of transitional
program participants? 59
Goal 2: Current Program Areas and Components,
Program Area and Component Importance, and
Program Outcomes 69
Question 3: What are the program areas and
components in current transitional programs? 69
Question 4: Where are program areas and
components provided? 78
Question 5: Who provides the program area and
component? 82
Question 6: What is the perceived importance of each
program area and component in transitional
programs? 86
Question 7: What are the current programs'
outcomes? 91
Goal 3: Program Demographics, Program Areas, and
Components Related to Successful Program
Outcomes and Important in an Effective
Transitional Program 93

Question 8: What are the demographics of programs
  with successful outcomes? 93
Question 9: Which program areas and components
  are present in programs with successful outcomes? 102
Question 10: Which program demographics, program
  area, and components are important in an effective
  transitional program model? 109

5. SUMMARY, CONCLUSIONS, AND
     RECOMMENDATIONS 117
  Summary 117
  Conclusions 118
    Description of Current Programs 118
    Profile of Current Transitional Program Participants 119
    Current Program Components 119
    Directors' Perceptions of Component Importance 120
    Current Program Outcomes 120
    Effective Transitional Program Demographics and
      Components 120
  Framework Recommendations 121
  Future Research 125

APPENDICES 127
  A. DEFINITIONS OF GOVERNMENT PROGRAMS
       AND LEGISLATION 127
  B. EXPERT PANEL REVIEW LETTER 137
  C. PRETEST COVER LETTER 139
  D. SURVEY COVER LETTER 141
  E. SURVEY QUESTIONNAIRE 143
  F. REMINDER POSTCARD 175
BIBLIOGRAPHY 177
INDEX 189

Tables

1.6	Data on Homeless Families in Cities with Transitional Programs Surveyed by the U.S. Conference of Mayors	5
4.1	Geographical Locations of Responding Transitional Programs	53
4.2	Program Directors' Descriptions of Their Programs	54
4.3	Number of Individual Family Living Units in Programs	54
4.4	Length of Program	55
4.5	Agencies and Other Organizations That Have Linkages With the Programs	56
4.6	Source of Funding for Programs	57
4.7	Types and Number of Participants in Responding Programs	59
4.8	Ages of Women with Children in Responding Programs	60
4.9	Race of Women With Children in Responding Programs	60
4.10	Marital Status of Women With Children in Responding Programs	61
4.11	Age of Children in Responding Programs	61
4.12	Reasons for Participants' Homelessness	63
4.13	Educational Level of Participants	65
4.14	Participants' Employment Status Before Entering the Program	65
4.15	Directors' Assessment of Participants' Employability	66
4.16	Reasons for the Unemployment of Participants	67

4.17 Program Areas and Components in Current Transitional
    Programs   70
4.18 Types of Case Management and Support Services
    Follow-up Available to Participants   74
4.19 When Case Management and Support Services Were
    Provided to Program Participants   75
4.20 Length of Follow-up Service   76
4.21 Level at Which Follow-up Was Funded   76
4.22 Types of Employment Training Provided in Programs   77
4.23 Number of Hours Spent Per Week in Employment
    Training   77
4.24 Job Placement Services Used in Programs   77
4.25 Where Program Areas and Components Were Provided   79
4.26 Educational Institutions Where Adult Basic Education
    Was Provided   81
4.27 Organizations Which Provided Employment Training   82
4.28 Program Area and Component Providers   83
4.29 Importance of Program Areas and Components   87
4.30 Current Program Outcomes   92
4.31 Demographic Data That Have a Relationship to
    Successful Program Outcomes   94
4.32 Programs Size's Relationship to Successful Program
    Outcomes: Program Size by Improved Educational
    Level   98
4.33 Components That Were Related to Program
    Description   99
4.34 Program Areas and Components That Were Related to
    Program Length   100
4.35 Components That Related to Number of Individual
    Family Living Units in the Program   101
4.36 Analysis of Variance of Number of Program
    Components in Each Program Area by Program
    Outcomes   104
4.37 Program Area and Components That Improve Program
    Outcomes: Component by Improved Educational
    Level   105
4.38 Components That Improve Program Outcomes:
    Component by Increased Residential Stability   108
4.39 Components That Improve Program Outcomes:
    Component by Improved Employment Status   111

4.40 Components That Improve Program Outcomes:
Component by Increased Income   112
4.41 Effective Program Areas, Components, and
Demographics   113
4.42 Components Perceived Important by 100% of Program
Directors   116
5.1 Program Framework   122

Acknowledgments

To Dr. William L. Thuemmel, my chair, thank you for your expertise, diligence, and guidance. To Dr. Kenneth A. Parker, thank you for your support and advice. Finally to Dr. Frank P. Lattuca, my mentor and colleague, thank you for being there to listen, offer advice, and provide encouragement.

I am deeply indebted to the transitional program directors, who generously agreed to share their time and expertise. I hope the findings can help the participants of your programs to succeed in becoming self-sufficient.

Thank you to my colleagues at the University of Massachusetts. Your support was greatly appreciated. Special thanks to Dr. Linda L. Lowry, who was always there to provide encouragement and advice; Linda S. Smith, M.L.A., my editor and writing advisor; and Dr. Atul Sheel, for his assistance with statistical analysis.

Thanks go to all my many friends who listened, encouraged, and helped with all the tedious tasks. Special thanks go to Dr. Dottie Bauer, Dr. Irene Foster, Sarah Nell Barnes, Fay Flanary, The Millers (Judith, Brian, and Jillian), and Jim and Joanne Tregaskis.

Special thanks to my family for your love and support. My parents, Rev. LeRoy and Joyce Flohr, encouraged me to keep on task, and lent a willing hand whenever needed. Barb, Mark, Sue, Dave, Kevin, and Lori provided encouragement and assistance of time, talent, and computer equipment. Gwen, Julie, Jason, Danielle, Trevor, and Jeremy provided hugs, kisses, and joy.

Transitional Programs
for Homeless Women
with Children

CHAPTER 1

Introduction

IMPORTANCE OF THE STUDY

Family homelessness is one of the most profound and disturbing social problems of the 1990's and will be one of the most important issues facing the United States in the twenty-first century. Family homelessness contradicts the essence of what one often thinks of as family life—a secure, sheltered place for nurturing children. Most homeless families are headed by single women who are victims of poverty; are disadvantaged by ethnic, educational, and income status; lack advanced education or job training; and are hampered by poor family functions in their family of origin.

Parenting is a challenging endeavor under the best of circumstances. Homeless women bear the burden of raising children under precarious conditions and are vulnerable to violent crimes, rape, sexually transmitted diseases, and substance abuse. Family structure and cohesion are tested by stresses of a homeless life and basic survival. The homeless families' struggles have immediate and long-term consequences for homeless children's development and affect the homeless women's capacity to function effectively as parents and productively as members of society. They do not have the life skills to cope with poverty. Most are second generation welfare recipients. They are poor children having poor children. This cycle of poverty must be broken. The Institute for Children and Poverty (1994) noted:

> Sadly, today's young homeless families may represent a new generation of welfare dependency, thus perpetuating a vicious cycle. With their limited access to education and employment opportunities,

coupled with severe and inter-generational poverty, a family's ability to better their lives appears nearly impossible. These same barriers to economic advancement and independent living become virtually unbreakable once families cross the threshold to homelessness. (p. 3)

Strengthening the mother is of primary importance so she can become self-sufficient and economically independent, and can positively impact her own child's development. The United States cannot afford to allow this cycle of family poverty and homelessness to continue. It is morally, ethically, and economically imperative that the multiple needs of the homeless family be addressed.

BACKGROUND

The fastest growing homeless group in the United States, since the late 1980s, is families with children (Bassuk & Buckner, 1994; Burt, 1992; DaCosta Nunez, 1994; Homes for the Homeless, 1998; Institute of Medicine, 1988; Lam, 1987; National Coalition for the Homeless, 1993; Rossi, 1994b; U.S. Conference of Mayors, 1987, 1993, 1994; Wright & Lam, 1987; Wright & Weber, 1987). The U.S. Conference of Mayors' annual survey is one of the few ongoing studies on hunger and homelessness in United States cities.

Selected data on homeless families and transitional programs in the 29 continental United States cities surveyed by the Conference of Mayors in 1994 are shown in Table 1.1. The data shown indicate the percentage of the city's homeless population that were categorized as homeless families, the percentage of the homeless families that were headed by a single parent and the number of family transitional individual living units in the city. Transitional units are individual family living spaces. Depending on a program's living space design, a unit may be anything from an individual family living/sleeping space with communal kitchen, dining, and recreation areas to individual family apartments. A unit is defined as the living space available for one family in the program. These data indicate that family homelessness was an issue in the selected cities and that transitional programs were available for the researcher to study.

Table 1.1: Data on Homeless Families in Cities with Transitional Programs Surveyed by the U.S. Conference of Mayors

City	Indicator		
	Homeless Families as a % of City's Homeless Population	% of Homeless Families Headed by a Single Parent	Number of Family Transitional Units in City
Alexandria	34	79	54
Boston	40	93	188
Charleston	30	93	4
Charlotte	37.6	95	32
Chicago	43	98.6	382
Cleveland	20	98.6	72
Denver	15	70	130
Detroit	28	99	7
Kansas City	62	84	N/A
Los Angeles	19	50	817
Louisville	34.4	N/A	115
Miami	42	90	25
Minneapolis	62	75	100
Nashville	16	70	89
New Orleans	18	88	89
New York City	74	N/A	4,132
Norfolk	17	96	7
Philadelphia	59.1	93	467
Portland	52	89	126
Providence	41	22	50-60
Saint Louis	66	68	528
Saint Paul	42	95	187
Salt Lake City	28	67	50
San Antonio	67	86	114
San Diego	26	80	240
San Francisco	25	4	141
Santa Monica	14	78	3
Seattle	27	59	N/A
Trenton	77	92	20

Note. N/A denotes that the information was not available. From U.S. Conference of Mayors, 1994.

The 1994 survey found that requests for shelter for homeless families alone increased by 21% from November 1, 1993 to October 31, 1994. Nine out of 10 cities in the survey reported an increase in requests for shelter from November 1, 1993 to October 31, 1994. Requests from all homeless persons, but particularly by homeless families for emergency shelter, were expected to increase in 71% of the cities in 1995 (U.S. Conference of Mayors, 1994). Twenty-five percent of all requests by homeless families went unmet between November 1, 1993 to October 31, 1994 (U.S. Conference of Mayors, 1994). Families with children were identified by 73% of the cities as a group of homeless people for whom shelter and other needed services are particularly lacking (U.S. Conference of Mayors, 1994). Shinn and Weitzman, (1996) found that families with children constitute 40% of people who became homeless, while on any given night, an estimated 20% of the homeless population were families. In 1997, the Conference of Mayor's study found that children accounted for 20% of the homeless in the 29 city survey (Waxman and Trupin, 1997).

Homelessness for this group is not simply a housing issue, but one of children, one of families, and one of education (DaCosta Nunez, 1994). In several United States cities, families make up over half of the homeless population (U.S. Conference of Mayors, 1994; (U.S. Conference of Mayors, 1997). They are victims of poverty, often unemployed mothers and children, who lack adequate education and job skills.

The National Coalition for the Homeless (1994) noted the following issues facing policy makers with respect to family homelessness: (a) long waiting lists for Section 8 rental subsidies and public housing; (b) the inappropriate placement of children into foster care because their families are homeless or have severe housing problems; (c) the shortage of emergency and transitional shelter with comprehensive services to help families move out of homelessness; and (d) the substantial minority of homeless children who are not attending school regularly.

Female-headed households with children are precisely the families most likely to become homeless. Seventy-eight percent of the homeless families in the U.S. Conference of Mayors' survey (1994) were headed by a single parent. The homeless families are usually headed by very young women raising their children on their own, usually without any form of child support from absent fathers. Households headed by women are more likely to be poor for several reasons—their lower earning capacity, greater poverty, greater reliance on non inflation-adjusted public welfare, and their conflicting role obligations and child care responsibilities that make it harder for them to work full-time (Burt, 1992; DaCosta Nunez, 1994).

These young women with children come from backgrounds that include foster care, substance abuse, domestic violence, inadequate health care, and poor education (Homes for the Homeless, 1998). They consistently lack basic social supports, such as family or community ties. Most have less than a high school education and little, if any, work experience (Homes for the Homeless, 1998). They are faced with the issue of child care as well as finding a job that will support the entire family, with few means to accomplish either. Burt and Cohen (1989) found that 35% of mothers in homeless families had held a steady job (3 or more months with the same employer) within the last 12 months before being interviewed, but 37% had not worked steadily for four years or more. They are limited to low paying, low-skilled jobs that can barely bring their families above the poverty line, let alone provide day care, health care, and decent housing.

In many cities, housing is available at reasonable cost, but because of unemployment or low wage rates, many households do not have enough income to afford even cheap housing. In these cities, one response would be to apply a range of remedies including housing subsidies, job development, retraining unemployed workers, supporting housing for the disabled, and expanding drug treatment capacity and viable alternatives to drug activity for the most vulnerable populations (Burt, 1992). The cities in the U.S. Conference of Mayors' (1994) survey identified raising the minimum wage, expanding job training, and creating additional jobs as the most important actions the federal government could take to address the income needs of the homeless people. Establishing a continuum of care was an important recommendation for addressing the service needs of homeless persons (U.S. Conference of Mayors, 1994). The most effective policy approaches will involve working with all the people in a household as a unit. As long as the issues of education and job training go unaddressed, these families stand at risk of repeated episodes of homelessness.

Revitalizing the American economy depends, in part, on producing an educated and well-trained work force that can participate in cooperative productive endeavors and respond to changing demands. Economic opportunity and mobility are generally tied directly to educational achievement. In today's job market, where information and service industries predominate, this is truer than ever. Employers in the 1990s require a higher level of education than in the past. The education system has failed most extremely with those who need training the most, and who are most vulnerable to homelessness. It is essential that public education be revitalized, especially for the poorest children; that more sophisticated job training and apprenticeship programs be developed; that greater cooperation between employers and educators be sought; and that employers be encouraged to invest in the continuous education and training of workers (Burt, 1992; Da Costa Nunez, 1994).

Burt and Cohen (1989) found that homeless women with children had little or no attachment to the labor force. For these low-skilled, low educated, low work-experience women with children, support for permanently leaving the homeless condition and becoming self-sufficient will include basic skills training, job readiness, job training, job search assistance, and training in parenting and life management skills (Burt & Cohen, 1989). Burt and Cohen (1989) also found that homeless women with children needed support in food assistance, medical care, and shelter acquisition.

The employment status of the homeless and their potential employability is of utmost importance in policy formation. Most homeless education and job training programs today neglect the needs of homeless women with children and are designed for homeless men, homeless single women, and the formerly homeless (DaCosta Nunez, 1994). Other types of job training programs specifically aimed at welfare recipients are inadequate for homeless women with children (Homes for the Homeless, 1996). The homeless women with children often begin at a much lower job-readiness level (Homes for the Homeless, 1996). They require more basic education and training than is typically offered. Many need supportive services unavailable in traditional programs, ranging from child care to assistance with permanent housing placement. Many facilities refer homeless women to job training programs when such programs are often inappropriate or inaccessible to homeless parents. Parent education and job training are generally ignored as subjects of homeless policy. Although some federal initiatives have begun to allocate funds for adult literacy, basic education, and job training, the programs tend to be limited and receive minimal allocations in the federal budget. The appropriateness of education and employment training programs for this population need to be explored (Da Costa Nunez, 1994; Lam, 1987).

PURPOSE OF THE STUDY

The main purpose of this study was to develop a transitional program framework that can assist homeless women with children to become self-sufficient. In order to create this framework; this study identified current program areas and components in transitional programs for homeless women with children, including education and employment training components; and determined which program areas and components of current programs have a relationship to programs with successful outcomes. The three goals of this study were:

1. To identify, characterize, and analyze the current transitional programs for homeless women with children.

2. To determine the current program areas and components, perceived program areas and component importance, and program outcomes.

3. To determine which program demographics, program areas, and components are related to successful program outcomes and are important in effective transitional programs.

RESEARCH QUESTIONS

The study will attempt to answer the following questions:

1. What are the profiles of the transitional programs for homeless women with children?

2. What are the profiles of transitional program participants?

3. What are the program areas and components in current transitional programs?

4. Where are the program areas and components provided?

5. Who provides the program areas and components?

6. What is the perceived importance of each program area and component in transitional programs?

7. What are the current programs outcomes?

8. What are the demographics of programs with successful outcomes?

9. Which program areas and components are present in programs with successful outcomes?

10. Which program demographics, program areas, and, components are important in an effective transitional program framework?

SIGNIFICANCE OF THE STUDY

The data from the survey will be used to develop a demographic profile of current programs and participants; an overview of current program areas, components, and outcomes; and a determination of the relationship of the identified program areas and components to effective transitional programs for homeless women with children. This information can then form the basis for a framework, which can be used by private organizations, educational institutions, and government agencies that develop policy and programs for homeless women with children. The descriptive data and data on program outcomes can guide the development of future program projects.

CHAPTER 2

Literature Review

DEFINITION OF HOMELESSNESS

The homeless are defined as primarily persons completely without shelter, those living in homeless shelters who would otherwise be without places in which to sleep, and those doubled up with others or in inappropriate housing as at-risk populations (Rossi, 1989a, 1994b). Those living in the shelters or on the streets and in other public places are considered the literal homeless. Persons living in conventional housing but either doubled up, tripled up, or on the verge of losing their housing are considered precariously housed (Rossi, 1994b). This suggests that today homelessness is considered primarily a housing problem (Rossi, 1994b).

The Stewart B. McKinney Homeless Assistance Act (Public Law 100-77, see Appendix A for further information), enacted in July 1987, defines homelessness as an individual who lacks a fixed, regular, and adequate nighttime residence; or an individual who has a primary nighttime residence that is (a) a supervised or publicly operated shelter designed to provide temporary living accommodations (including welfare hotels, congregate shelters, and transitional housing for the mentally ill); (b) an institution that provides a temporary residence for individuals intended to be institutionalized; or (c) a public or private place not designed for, or ordinarily used as, a regular sleeping accommodation for human beings. This definition is applicable to individuals and homeless families (National Coalition for the Homeless, 1988b).

Patterns of homelessness are usually categorized in the following ways:

1. Temporary homelessness arises when people are displaced from their usual dwellings by natural or man-made calamities.

2. Episodically homeless people are those who frequently go in and out of homelessness and comprise the majority of homeless individuals today. They are primarily persons living in poverty whose month-to-month finances are precarious and for whom short-term reversals of fortune result in episodes of homelessness in varying severity and duration (Rossi, 1989b). As long as there is a poverty population whose incomes put them on the economic edge and no social welfare system to protect them against short term economic difficulties, there will be persons who fall into the state of homelessness. A large portion of this population consists of young female-headed households in transition from one household to another, using shelters as a resting place until they can establish a new home on their own, often while waiting for certification as Aid to Families with Dependent Families (AFDC) recipients (see Appendix A for further information).

3. Chronic homelessness occurs when people have spent more than a year on the streets without any intervening period of residential stability. These long-term homeless have disabilities of all types that impair their earning power, diminish their employment prospects, and reduce their acceptance by families, kin, and friends. This group is most affected by shortages in unskilled jobs, by loss of inexpensive housing, and by declines in the economic fortunes of their social networks (Rossi, 1989b).

NUMBERS OF HOMELESS

Scholars and government agencies have been working to develop reliable methods of analyzing the numbers of homeless because the present numbers are more informed impressions rather than confirmed findings. The dispute over the number of homeless people is tied up in the definition of homeless that is chosen (Lam, 1987; Liebow, 1993; Rossi, 1989a). Depending on whether one adopts a narrow or broad definition, the number of homeless will be affected by orders of magnitude (Rossi, 1989b). But there is agreement among most researchers and advocacy groups that the numbers have increased since the early 1980s (Burt, 1992; Institute of Medicine, 1988; National Coalition for the Homeless, 1993; Rossi, 1989a). Burt and Cohen (1989) developed what is considered the best existing estimate—500,000 homeless people in the United States. For the purpose of this study, the question of precisely how many homeless people there are is not of central importance because homelessness is not static; poor women with children move in and out of a state of homelessness.

CHARACTERISTICS OF THE HOMELESS

Many of the homeless studies have focused on the demographic, social, and health characteristics of homeless adults living in large cities or wider geographic rural areas. The data collected have shown similarities—although sites at which data were collected, sampling strategy, and operational criteria, differed. The homeless are for the most part drawn from the ranks of the poverty population (Burt, 1992; Lam, 1987; Liebow, 1993; DaCosta Nunez, 1994; National Coalition for the Homeless, 1993, 1998; Rossi, 1989b; Wright, 1989; Wright & Weber, 1987). Studies have shown few differences between homeless people and other very poor people (Burt, 1992; Liebow, 1993). Homelessness is not a new phenomenon. From World War II to the present, the homeless population has consisted mainly of young transient males looking for work and older alcoholic men living on skid rows. These groups have been joined by the "new homeless," and it is the latter group that is responsible for the increased visibility of, and public concern for, the homeless. The number of homeless has increased dramatically and the composition of the homeless population has changed during the last decade (Burt, 1992; Institute of Medicine, 1988; Lam, 1987; DaCosta Nunez, 1994; Rossi, 1989b; Wright, 1989; Wright & Weber, 1987).

The "new homeless" are younger (early 20s), are dominated by a more racially and ethnically diverse population, include the deinstitutionalized mentally ill, and are increasingly more likely to be members of families (Institute of Medicine, 1988; Lam, 1987; DaCosta Nunez, 1994; Rossi, 1989b; Wright & Lam, 1987; Wright, 1989; Wright & Weber, 1987). Children under the age of 18, usually part of a family headed by a mother, are the fastest growing component of the homeless population (DaCosta Nunez, 1994; Homes for the Homeless 1998: Institute of Medicine, 1988; Lam, 1987; National Coalition for the Homeless, 1993; U.S. Conference of Mayors, 1987, 1993, 1994,

1997; Wright & Lam, 1987; Wright & Weber, 1987). The elderly are underrepresented among the homeless in comparison with their percentage in the general population (Institute of Medicine, 1988, Rossi, 1989b; Wright, 1989).

The characteristics of the homeless population differ from one community to another (Burt & Cohen, 1989; Rossi, 1989a). Rossi (1989a) noted that ethnic composition of the homeless is heavily influenced by the ethnic composition of the community under study. Rural residents have a long tradition of preferring self-help and reliance on relatives, friends, and neighbors instead of taxpayer-supported programs, which has effectively disguised the magnitude of the problem of rural homelessness. The rural homeless appear slightly younger than their urban counterparts and more likely to be living in intact, two-parent families in which both parents were recently employed before being forced into poverty and homelessness (Institute of Medicine, 1988). There are more homeless two-parent families in the West and Southwest than in New York and other large eastern cities (U.S. Conference of Mayors, 1987). The homeless tend to be long-term residents of the city in which they live (Institute of Medicine, 1988; Wright, 1989). Urban and rural families usually have gone through several stages of doubling up with family and friends before becoming visibly homeless (Institute of Medicine, 1988).

The homeless are relatively isolated socially. The homeless have few enduring and supporting ties to family, friends, and kin (Burt, 1992; Rossi, 1994b, 1989a; Wright, 1989). Sometimes this was caused by family disruption and friction. Garrett and Bahr (1973) define this state as disaffiliation. Burt (1992) noted that this population was twice as likely to have lived in out-of-home institutions as children. In the Homes of the Homeless report *For Whom the Bell Tolls* (1997) it is noted evidence that 50% of the homeless mothers were introduced to America's institutions of support as children. Burt (1992) noted:

> This finding signals a probable breakdown or incapacity of their family of origin while they were still children. . . . Moreover, lack of family network increases an already rather high risk of homelessness, as does behavior that strains one's relationship with family, such as alcohol abuse. (p. 58)

Alcohol and drug abuse, physical disabilities, and mental illness, or a combination of these problems (co-morbidity) are the major health issues of the homeless adult population (Institute of Medicine, 1988; Lam, 1987; Rossi, 1989a; Wright, 1989; Wright & Weber, 1987). The new homeless tend to be unskilled and are more likely to be unemployed, which results in lower incomes (Burt, 1992; DaCosta Nunez, 1994, Rossi, 1989b).

THE CAUSES OF HOMELESSNESS

There is rarely one reason why a person becomes homeless. The ways in which housing markets, employment, income, public benefit programs, and deinstitutionalization interact to produce and perpetuate homelessness are complex and vary with the individual. Those who end up on the street have typically had all the disadvantages. Most started life in families with a multitude of problems; many came from families so troubled that they were placed in foster care. Many had serious health and learning problems. A large number grew up in destitute neighborhoods and attended mediocre schools. After that, most had more than their share of bad luck in the labor market, in family formation, or both. It is the cumulative effect of all these disadvantages and the combination of personal vulnerability and political indifference that has left people in the streets (Burt, 1992; Jencks, 1994; DaCosta Nunez, 1994).

A number of factors in combination probably precipitate most episodes of homelessness. The causes can be divided into structural and personal categories. Structural factors refer to large-scale social and economic determinants that influence the well-being of the United States population, including the quality of housing. Personal factors include variables such as alcohol and drug abuse, mental illness, or social disaffiliation that determine an individual's ability to compete for scarce resources within the larger sociological-economic structure (Burt, 1992; Lam, 1987; Jencks, 1994; Rossi, 1989a; Wright, 1989; Wright & Weber, 1987).

There are four factors generally cited as causes of the rise and continued growth of homelessness. These factors focus on structural changes in American society. They are:

1. The continuing decimation of the low-cost housing stock in urban America along with the failure to fund construction of more low-cost housing during the same time as the poverty population of cities increased (Burt, 1992; DaCosta Nunez, 1994; Golden, 1992; Institute of Medicine, 1988; Kozol, 1988;

Lam 1987; Liebow, 1993; National Coalition for the Homeless, 1993; Rossi, 1989a; Salerno, Hopper, & Baxter, 1984; Wright, 1989; Wright & Lam, 1987; Wright, 1989; Wright & Weber, 1987).

2. A second factor that has contributed to the rise in homelessness was the economic recession of the early 1980s, accompanied by a rise in unemployment and structural changes in employment from a manufacturing to a service economy (Burt, 1992; Golden, 1992; Lam, 1987; National Coalition for the Homeless, 1993; Rossi, 1989a; Salerno, Hopper, & Baxter, 1984). This factor has caused a decline in unskilled and low-skilled labor employment opportunities. The majority of the new homeless consists of more or less permanently unemployed central city minority young males and females who have minimal educational credentials and uncertain work histories, which compound employment difficulties. Many of the young women are also mothers of young children, which adds additional employment problems (Lam, 1987; Salerno, Hopper, & Baxter, 1984).

3. Federal budget cuts to entitlement programs and programs aimed at preventing and breaking the cycle of poverty are implicated in the increase of homelessness (Burt, 1992; DaCosta Nunez, 1994; Golden, 1992; Institute of Medicine, 1988; Lam, 1987; National Coalition for the Homeless, 1993; Rossi, 1989a, 1994b; Salerno, Hopper, & Baxter, 1984).

4. The final factor cited in the growth of homelessness is the deinstitutionalization of the chronically mentally ill and the resultant practice of non-institutionalization (Burt, 1992; DaCosta Nunez, 1994; Golden, 1992; Institute of Medicine, 1988; Jencks, 1994; Lam, 1987; National Coalition for the Homeless, 1993; Salerno, Hopper, & Baxter, 1984; Rossi, 1989a; Wright, 1989; Wright & Weber, 1987).

Demographic changes in the United States population represent another seldom cited but important factor contributing to homelessness. The aging of the baby boom generation (persons born in the years between 1945 and 1965) has caused stiff competition for scarce resources of housing, jobs, and government aid that has pushed some people onto the street. The new homeless fall into the age category of the majority of baby boomers (Lam, 1987; Rossi, 1989a; Wright & Weber, 1987). Personal causes of homelessness include alcohol and drug abuse, mental illness, family rejection and dissolution of a marriage, and social disaffiliation (Golden; 1992; Jencks, 1994; Lam, 1987; Liebow, 1993).

Burt (1992), in her research of cities with a population of 100,000 or more, found that some other variables that tended to increase homelessness were (a) the city's population change (loss, stagnation, or growth), which is also a reflection of its economic fortunes; (b) the city's proportion of one-person households; (c) the absence of General Assistance; and (d) the cost of living for city residents.

HOMELESS WOMEN WITH CHILDREN

Historical Overview

In all time periods, people without permanent dwelling places have been considered homeless. Generally in American history the homeless have been transients, tramps, and the wandering poor traveling from rural areas to towns to cities in search of employment and housing. In the earlier part of the eighteenth century, the tramps were the traveling poor, nuclear families, women, and children moving in search of work. Tramping in the nineteenth century was the story of mass population movement caused by industrial transformation of the urban United States (Monkkonen, 1984). Cyclical unemployment and economic crises directly caused the most prominent periods of tramping (Lam, 1987). Single men tramped first; then if things continued to be bad, older married men with families became tramps. Only in the preindustrial period and during the Great Depression did whole families tramp. Tramps were the ordinary working people of the United States on the move between jobs and residences (episodically homeless). The disappearance of the industrial tramp occurred in the new world of the social welfare states, World War II, and the prosperity of the post-war years. The welfare state programs included social security, unemployment benefits, workers' compensation, various forms of subsidized medical care, and the disappearance of the ideological notion that to be effective welfare must be dispensed in the controlled environment of an institution.

In the twentieth century, the homeless include both transients and locals with perhaps the majority being from the city or state in which they are currently homeless (Institute of Medicine, 1988; Rossi, 1989b;

Wright, 1989). In the mid-1970s, researchers began to see a marked change in the character of homelessness. The decade was plagued with a recession that caused high unemployment levels, rising inflation, declining real wages, and a retrenchment in government programs that cushioned earlier economic downturns (Burt, 1992; Golden, 1992; Institute of Medicine, 1988; Lam, 1987; DaCosta Nunez, 1994; Rossi, 1989b; Rossi, 1994b; Salerno, Hopper, & Baxter, 1984).

During the recession of 1981-1982, emergency shelters and soup kitchens began reporting an increasing demand for their services. Even when economic conditions improved after 1983, homelessness continued to rise (Burt, 1992). During these three years, the homeless population grew 22% (Burt & Cohen, 1989). New groups seen in the homeless population included homeless women with children and more persons with mental illness and substance abuse problems. During the recession of 1981-1982, the presence of families with children among those seeking housing and food assistance was noted as a distinct change and was viewed as a sign of how deeply the recession had hurt poor households. Unemployed fathers' only hope of supporting their families was desertion, which then resulted in their families' eligibility for Aid to Families with Dependent Children (AFDC).

The major theoretical concern in studying the homeless women was the societal-level changes that had occurred in the past 20-25 years leading to the increase in homeless women on the streets. This number has increased from zero around World War II to 25-30% of the homeless population in the early 1990s. The studies of the old skid rows found virtually no women in flophouses or on the streets. Studies in the 1980s found that one-quarter or more of the new homeless are women (Lam, 1987, Rossi, 1989a). This was a much higher proportion than found in studies before 1970. The information on homeless women since the late 1970s indicates that the middle-aged, single, disaffiliated, alcoholic, or mentally ill women have not disappeared. They have been joined by younger women who are more likely to be minorities, have dependent children, and be homeless for shorter periods of time. Women's personal incomes were rising, but their other main source of economic support, namely marriage, was in decline (Jencks, 1994). The fact that unskilled women with extremely low incomes not only married less but continued to have children pushed more of them into the streets (Jencks, 1994). By 1987, about 10% of the homeless households included children. Eight out of 10 of these family households were headed by a single women; all were very poor (Burt &

Cohen, 1989). In 1969, 16% of all unmarried working-age women with extremely low personal incomes had a child. By 1979, the figure was 23 %, and by 1989, it was 31%. The effect of this change was accentuated by the fact that more poor single mothers were living on their own. In both 1969 and 1979, half of all single mothers with personal income below $2,500 were living with at least one other adult. By 1989, the proportion was down to 36% (Jencks, 1994).

Economic and Social Factors

A number of economic and social forces have contributed to the homeless condition of these women. Women, in the past 25 years, have made up an increasing proportion of the poor. This is known as the "feminization of poverty." The reasons for the feminization of poverty are both structural and demographic. In the late 1970s, Sociologist Diane Pearce (1987) declared that poverty was becoming a female issue. In 1977, two-thirds of all poor persons 16 and over were women, and women comprised half of all poor household heads. The following four factors have contributed independently or in combination to the feminization of poverty.

The structural factors include the following:

1. Labor market factors such as gender differences in wages and occupational segregation. A sex-segregated labor market has evolved with women concentrated in low-paying jobs with little room for advancement.

2. Government income transfers, the scope and adequacy of public benefits and services for women and their families to redress their inequality in the labor market or for income lost or reduced as a result of their parental responsibilities, was the second main factor. In order to receive AFDC in many states, an adult male could not be present in the household, effectively driving away a potential wage earner. Welfare payments were often the only form of income available to women on their own, especially the elderly or single women with dependent children. These payments provided an income below the poverty income level.

3. Policies that did not adequately promote economic equality, such as equal pay legislation and affirmative action.

4. Demographic factors included rates of divorce, decline of household formation rates, rising teen birth rates, young women living alone longer due to later age of marriage, growing numbers of elderly women due to increasing longevity, and women simply choosing to live on their own more often than in the past have affected the proportion of all households headed by women (Goldberg & Kremen, 1987; Jencks, 1994; Lam, 1987, Pierce, 1987). Racism was also found to be a factor (Golden, 1992; Jencks, 1994; Liebow, 1993; Pierce, 1987). Over one-half of African-American women who were female head of households were poor, compared to a little over one-fourth of white women who were heads of households (Goldberg & Kremen, 1987).

There was a dramatic rise in the divorce rate (Jencks, 1994). Divorce can be financially devastating, especially for women. The decline of family formation left more women fending for themselves. The fact that fewer women have husbands seems to have especially increased homelessness among children, since men seldom do much to support their children unless they live under the same roof, and unskilled women can seldom support themselves and their children on their earnings alone (Jencks, 1994).

The abrupt rise of female-headed households was also a result of the uncertain economic fate of young men, especially young nonwhite men. Young men facing economic uncertainties became less attractive as mates, less willing to take the chances involved in becoming a head of household, and less abled to fulfill the economic role of husband and father when marriage and family formation do take place (Rossi, 1989a).

Profile of Homeless Women with Children

Homeless families have been identified as the fastest growing segment of the homeless population since 1987 (Burt, 1992; DaCosta Nunez, 1994; Homes for the Homeless 1998; Institute of Medicine, 1988; Lam, 1987; National Coalition for the Homeless, 1993; U.S. Conference of Mayors, 1987, 1993, 1994, 1997; Wright & Lam, 1987; Wright & Weber, 1987). In the 30 cities surveyed by the U.S. Conference of Mayors in 1994, 39% of the homeless were members of homeless families (U.S. Conference of Mayors, 1994). In the western regions, there were more intact homeless families than in the eastern regions

(Bassuk et al., 1986; McChesney, 1987). Homeless families with both parents were more common in rural areas than urban areas. In theory, any family that falls on hard times could become homeless. In practice, the problem is largely confined to single mothers. Single mothers are much poorer than married couples. That means they are more likely to become homeless. The women heading these families had difficulty establishing themselves as autonomous adults, they were unable to hold jobs, and generally lacked or have limited relationships with other adults or institutions. They were unable to maintain a home because of economic and interpersonal problems and had long histories of residential instability. This subgroup was the most likely to be long-term AFDC recipients, and their children could be the next generation of system dependent homeless adults (Bassuk, Rubin, & Lauriat, 1986). The Institute on Children and Poverty (1994) and Homes for the Homeless (1997) found that homeless women on AFDC were relatively new to the welfare system but that over 50% of them had grown up receiving support from America's institutions of support. Less than 30% of non-homeless AFDC recipients had grown up on General Assistance (for further information on AFDC and General Assistance see Appendix A).

Findings in studies of homeless families are generally descriptive, and there are large regional differences, but most supported the following generalizations about the characteristics and needs of homeless women with children:

1. Women were more likely than men to be part of the family group members and tended to be in their late 20s (Bassuk et al., 1986; McChesney, 1987), but some of the latest research is showing that the average age is in the early 20s (DaCosta Nunez, 1994).

2. Their ethnic composition tends to mirror the ethnic composition of the area where they live. These women were more likely than any other homeless group to be a member of a minority group (Burt, 1992).

3. They have completed at least several years of high school (Bassuk et al., 1986; McChesney, 1987).

4. A majority of the women are recipients of Aid to Families with Dependent Children (AFDC), Food Stamps (FSP), and General Assistance (GA) (Burt, 1992; DaCosta Nunez, 1994; Lam,

1987; Rossi, 1989a, 1994b). See Appendix A for more information on these programs.

The homeless women usually had two to three children (Burt, 1992; Bassuk, Rubin, & Lauriat, 1986; DaCosta Nunez, 1994; Jencks, 1994; Lam, 1987). Most of the children were under the age of five and were spending their critical development years without the stability and security of a permanent home (Bassuk et al.,1986; DaCosta Nunez; Wright & Weber, 1987). Most of the children manifested delayed development, serious symptoms of depression and anxiety, or learning problems (Bassuk & Rubin, 1987; Bassuk & Rosenberg, 1988; DaCosta Nunez, 1994; Wright, 1989).

The women were either single or divorced (Bassuk et al., 1986; McChesney, 1987). They were typically isolated and had few supportive relationships. Most of the women could not call on their own immediate families for support (Bassuk et al., 1986; McChesney, 1987). Many of the women were victims of family violence (Bassuk et al., 1986; DaCosta Nunez, 1994; Homes for the Homeless, 1998, Lam, 1987; Rossi, 1989a, 1994b, Waxman and Trupin, 1997). A Ford Foundation study found that 50% of homeless women with children are fleeing abuse (Schneider, 1990). Rossi (1989a) found that many of the women had fled a domestic situation so unacceptable that a life of homelessness became the preferred alternative.

The women had histories of residential instability and moved several times prior to their current shelter stay; most moved within the community they were sheltered. The majority of the women had doubled-up in overcrowded apartments and with friends and relatives, while others had previously resided in other shelters or welfare hotels (Bassuk et al, 1986). A substantial proportion of homeless families using the shelter system were characterized as multi-problem families (Bassuk et al., 1986). They faced chronic economic, educational, vocational, and social problems; had fragmented support networks; and had difficulty accessing the traditional service delivery system (Institute of Medicine, 1988).

Causes of family homelessness included economic housing factors such as a shortage of low-income housing, subsistence living by government supports such as the inadequacy of AFDC benefits, psychosocial factors such as the breakdown of the family structure in association with poverty, psychological deprivation, impoverished self-esteem, disruption, stress, and violence (Bassuk, et al., 1986; Burt,

1992; DaCosta Nunez, 1994; Golden, 1992; Homes for the Homeless, 1998; Jencks 1994; Lam, 1987; Liebow, 1993; Rossi, 1989a, 1994b, Waxman and Trupin, 1997).

PROFILE OF EMERGENCY AND TRANSITIONAL SHELTERS/HOUSING

The first initiative taken by the United States government in response to homelessness was the Emergency Food and Shelter Program contained in the Hobbs Stimulus Act of 1983 (Public Law 98-8). This program is administered by the Federal Emergency Management Administration (FEMA) and is run through a national board of nonprofit agencies that have extensive experience in programs for the homeless. In 1983, three-fourths of the resources of this program went toward food assistance; by 1989, more than half of the resources were committed to shelter services.

Emergency shelters admit families for a limited period of time and provide basic shelter needs for families who have lost their housing or are in imminent risk of losing their housing. These needs may include food, shelter, and health care. The federal government has become involved in services for the homeless, mainly in the area of financial support for shelters. Individuals, religious congregations, charitable organizations, the United Way, businesses, and foundations provide most of the labor, goods, and services.

Federal funds are available through the Stewart B. McKinney Homeless Assistance Act and account for the increase in federal government support, since late 1987. The U.S. Department of Housing and Urban Development (HUD) has an Emergency Shelter Grants (ESG) Program. This program is authorized under Title IV, Subtitle A, Stewart B. McKinney Homeless Assistance Act of 1987, as amended, Public Law 102-550. The program provides grants to states, metropolitan cities, urban counties, and territories according to the formula used for Community Development Block Grants (CDBG). The program is designed to help improve the quality of existing emergency shelters for the homeless, to make available additional shelters, to meet the costs of operating shelters and of providing essential social service to homeless individuals, and to help prevent homelessness. Further information on these government programs can be found in Appendix. A.

In 1994, 30% of all shelters, or approximately 1,900 shelters nationwide, were family shelters (Rossi, 1994b). Forty-one percent of these shelters have been started since 1984 (Rossi, 1994b). Families with children were identified by over 75% of the cities surveyed by the U.S. Conference of Mayors (1994) as the group of homeless people for whom shelter and other services are particularly lacking. Most family shelters specialize in providing quasi-private quarters for family groups, usually in one or two rooms per family with shared bathrooms and cooking facilities. In many cities, welfare departments provide temporary housing for families by renting rooms in hotels and motels, especially when no family shelter space is available. In some cities, this arrangement is increasing (Gallager, 1986; Ross, 1989a). The rents paid by the welfare departments for the rooms often exceed current rents at the lowest end of the housing market, and by a substantial margin (Gallagher, 1986; Kozol, 1988; Rossi, 1989a).

Transitional shelters/housing programs provide longer-term accommodations that tend to be closer to those provided in conventional housing. Transitional programs help people already homeless to get back into permanent housing, and most importantly to develop a greater capacity for self-sufficiency. Transitional programs frequently involve basic education and literacy training, job training, chemical dependency treatment, mental health treatment, home and money management training, child care, transportation, and other specialized services. Such services require substantially higher cash investments than do emergency services. These programs are still in their infancy and serve only a fraction of homeless individuals and families but are currently considered an important part of the continuum of care. The structures and activities of transitional programs are limited only by the ingenuity of the service providers who directly observe the needs of their participants and work to create supportive programs and services tailored to those needs.

The U.S. Department of Housing and Urban Development's Supportive Housing Demonstration Program (SHDP) was authorized under Title IV, subtitle C, of the Stewart B. McKinney Homeless Assistance Act of 1987, as amended (see Appendix A for further information). The program was designed to promote the development of supportive housing and supportive services, including innovative approaches to assist homeless persons in the transition from homelessness and to enable them to live as independently as possible. One of the Supportive Housing Demonstration Program's (SHDP) two programs was the Transitional Housing Program (TH). Funds were used to provide transitional housing designed to enable homeless persons and families to move to permanent housing within a 24-month period, which may include up to six months of follow-up services after the resident moves to permanent housing. This temporary housing was combined with supportive services to enable homeless individuals to live as independently as possible. Supportive services help to promote residential stability, to increase skill levels and or income, and to promote greater self-determination. The program outcomes included increased residential stability, increased educational level, improved employment status, increased income, and greater self-determination (Office of Policy Development and Research, 1995). The services were provided by the organization managing the housing or coordinated by them and provided by other public or private agencies. Transitional housing was provided at a central facility or in leased units with rental assistance. In 1995, the status of this program changed from demonstration projects to a funded program call the Supportive Housing Program (SHP). Funds are awarded on the basis of competitive grants to cities and other organizations. These funds were part of The Housing Choice and Community Investment Act of 1994. Three thousand applications were received for the 900 million dollars in homeless assistance grants in 1995. These monies were awarded to cities and organizations who provided a comprehensive coordination of services with a continuum of care. The fundamental components of a continuum of care system are:

1. An emergency shelter/assessment effort that provides immediate shelter and can identify an individual's or family's needs.

2. Transitional housing and necessary social services;

3. Permanent housing or permanent supportive housing arrangements.

These programs would replace the feeding programs and emergency shelters with programs that address the specific needs of the homeless individual and family. These needs include job training, counseling, substance abuse counseling and other services that help the homeless move to permanent housing. These services are provided by various community collaboratives between government agencies, non-profit providers and other organizations (United States Department of Housing and Urban Development, 1995).

Rossi (1994b) notes the following critical functions performed by homeless family shelters:

- The emergency homeless shelter provides a bottom layer to local housing markets, providing essential rent-free accommodations to families who might otherwise be completely shelterless. Families at imminent risk of losing their housing are provided with interim housing on their way to other accommodations.

- Shelters also provide means by which families can leave intolerable living arrangements without exposing children to the very real physical and psychological dangers of being shelterless for any period of time.

- Service-rich transitional shelters not only avert the shelterless condition but provide socialization experiences through therapy and education that may help client families to better survive housing crises in the future. (p. 382)

The magnitude and nature of the problems of homelessness are so unprecedented that there are few past experiences that could guide planning efforts by public officials and community agencies. Adequate services must be provided, but without permanently institutionalizing homeless families through another human resource system that inherently provides second-class services. Better housing is still the first step in dealing with the problem. Regardless of why people are on the streets, giving them a place to live that offers a modicum of privacy and stability is usually the most important thing that can be done to improve their lives.

EDUCATION AND EMPLOYMENT TRAINING

Employment

Studies have found that 55% of the homeless had looked for employment in the previous month (Urban Institute as cited in Nation Commission for Employment Policy, 1990). A Massachusetts study found that 87% of parents in a shelter named a job or career as their major goal or dream in life (Hemminger & Quinones, 1992). Liebow (1993) found that when homeless women speak about themselves in relation to work, they almost always identify themselves as working, as looking for work, or as one who would work if she could. They considered a job the way out of homelessness.

An individual's identity as well as social life is tied to his or her job. To be engaged in a task that the community says is useful is the principal way one earns a living and becomes a valued member of that community. Jobs are a principal source of both independence and connectedness to others. The demoralizing and debilitating effects of long-term unemployment may lead to depression, mental anxieties, and alcohol and drug use (Rossi, 1989a). Because they cannot find steady jobs, they cannot afford to internalize the work ethic or link their self-respect to their job performance. Underemployment undermines the work ethic, as do jobs that lead nowhere, and jobs that do not pay enough to live on (Burt, 1992; Liebow, 1993; Jencks, 1994; Rossi, 1989a).

For homeless people, the road to looking for, finding, and keeping a job is strewn with obstacles. Most of the homeless have characteristics that make them the last hired and first fired. Having no telephone where a prospective employer or employment agency can reach you during working hours is often reason enough to discourage prospective employers and agencies from wanting to hire the homeless person. The person who confesses to having no telephone of one's own, or even access to one, is suspect. Women reported losing jobs or the opportunity to get them when their homelessness became known (Liebow, 1993). The women must make a minimally decent and unremarkable appearance, which includes cleanliness, neatness, and lack of body odor. For most women living in shelters, this may require a special effort. The homeless women also need planning and organizing skills that are scarce, especially among a largely impoverished and sometimes demoralized population (Liebow, 1994).

A deterrent to job seeking was the fact that, in strict economic terms, low-paying jobs were not clearly superior to public assistance. To leave public assistance usually means to forfeit food stamps and medical assistance. Permanent full-time jobs at entry-level positions typically offer health coverage only after a probationary period of anywhere from two to six months, sometimes such coverage is prohibitively costly and employees decline it. Many times the women can only get jobs as part-time workers, self-employed workers, or independent contract workers. In these types of jobs, the employees are not regular employees and therefore receive no benefits, health coverage, or job security. Other reasons for not taking jobs or keeping them involved things like fear of failure, embarrassment, or other risks to one's self-image.

Single mothers now care for their children. If they become employed, someone else will have to care for their children while they are at work. In addition, when single mothers work, they need even more income because they now have to pay for transportation to work, appropriate workplace clothing, child care, and medical care. Their jobs may not provide medical insurance, and even those that do usually expect workers to pay a large part of the cost.

Education and Job Training

Efforts to prevent homelessness must do something substantial about the poverty and low earnings potential that underlies the problem (Burt, 1992). Lam's (1987) data suggested that job training, placement, and counseling programs for the homeless women would be useful for one-fourth of this group. Twenty percent of homeless women were not employable because of lack of job skills and education. Lam (1987) suggested that this homeless population could benefit from job skills training and education, especially homeless women with children.

The types of women that are considered non-employable have problems such as mental illness, alcoholism, and physical disorders. These women are not amenable to job training programs, but sheltered workshops in conjunction with treatment programs may be an employment alternative.

A growing majority of homeless heads-of-households lack the basic qualifications necessary for a job that provides for a family. They were affected by cuts to education funding. Since the 1980s, federal support to elementary and secondary schools has fallen by one-third. Hardest hit were poorer school districts with insufficient property-tax revenues to make up the difference. Higher dropout rates and poorer achievement levels among low-income children attest to these disparities (DaCosta Nunez, 1994). These young homeless women need skills that will enable them to secure stable and gainful employment. Low-income parents also encounter barriers that prevent participation in programs. These barriers include transportation, scheduling, and lack of adequate child care (DaCosta Nunez, 1994).

Some education and training programs are too limited, reaching few of those in need. Other programs have unrealistic expectations and preparation. Many programs do not provide for a changing job market or economic climate and often leave participants without the flexibility to adapt. Job training programs often neglect to prepare the participant for the disappointments of the job search and the rigors of full-time employment.

Homeless women with children suffer from a severe, chronic form of poverty that places the women outside the scope of traditional job training programs. Even job training programs specifically aimed to welfare recipients are inadequate for homeless women with children (Homes for the Homeless, 1996; Institute for Children and Poverty, 1994). These women often begin at a much lower job-readiness level or lack the ability to meet the minimum requirement of a job training program. Programs for this population must address more than job skills and provide more basic education and job readiness training than is typically offered (Homes for the Homeless, 1996). Many need supportive services unavailable in traditional programs such as child care, medical care, transportation, and assistance to permanent housing. Many facilities refer homeless women to job training, when such programs are often inappropriate or inaccessible to homeless parents. Some programs avoid serving homeless clients. In a study of 55 urban Job Training Partnership Act (JTPA) programs, two-thirds offered no services aimed at addressing the multiple needs of homeless women with children (National Commission of Employment Policy, 1990).

EDUCATION AND JOB TRAINING PROGRAMS

For 1995, fifteen million dollars were authorized by the McKinney Act and related programs for education and job training programs (National Coalition for the Homeless, 1994). Recently support for the McKinney Act programs especially education and job training programs for the homeless have decreased or been eliminated. The long-term reduction of extreme poverty involves radically improving the labor market opportunities for young people. Education improves the chances of the homeless to get or keep jobs, improve the quality of their life, or ultimately provide shelter for themselves and their families. Most homeless persons have weaknesses in basic skills and literacy. Knowledge, awareness, and basic literacy skills can help the homeless to improve their present conditions, expand their choices, and learn to cope in today's world.

One of the National Coalition for the Homeless (1993) recommendations to Congress was to expand and strengthen federal employment policy. The Coalition suggested establishing a federally funded but locally administered public works program. The employment and training programs would be targeted to those least likely to be competitive in today's economy. The new initiatives would address the immediate need for work and the long-term need for an educated labor force.

Improving the job prospects for young women cannot help but bring improvements in the situation of a majority of the extremely poor, who are women heading their own households. Providing employment may lower the proportion of the very young women electing motherhood as an occupation. Having job experience would make it easier for women to enter the job market after their children are older. A consistent finding in evaluations is that job-training programs have proved more effective in improving the long-term economic condition of women trainees (Rossi, 1989a).

For homeless parents, the biggest obstacle to employment is lack of support. Training for and obtaining a job is not enough. Evidence suggests that job training and education programs for low-income people, or "welfare to work" programs, cannot be widely effective unless participants are supported in their personal and family lives. Child care and transitional family income support are among the most important requirements for success. There is a considerable body of evidence demonstrating the benefits to disadvantaged and disorganized families of intensive family-orientated services. Such approaches are characterized by flexibility in meeting the families' multiple needs and by specific aids, such as developmental day-care programs, infant stimulation programs, and Head Start programs; parental counseling; education; and job training. Such intensive intervention efforts are expensive to begin with but have cost effective benefits in the long run (Schorr, 1988). Those programs with the greatest promise are integrated and intensive forms of skills training and education, combined with a strong network of support services (Institute for Children and Poverty, 1994; DaCosta Nunez, 1994; Institute of Medicine, 1988).

Manpower Training Programs

If the private labor market is unable to provide sufficient employment opportunities to able young people, then the federal government may resort to public-sector employment. Some of the public employment programs in United States history include the Civilian Conservation

Corps (CCC), Works Progress Administration (WPA), Comprehensive Employment Training Act of 1973 (CETA), Job Corps, and Job Training Partnership Act of 1982 (JTPA). See Appendix A for further information on these programs.

Public employment programs are preferable to income maintenance programs in terms of human values because they mitigate both the demoralizing effects of unemployment and the stigma of welfare. The programs provide earned income and job activities to persons who would have none. The overhead costs might exceed the corresponding costs of simple transfer-payment system programs, but the benefits to participants cannot be obtained in straight cash payouts.

Job Training Partnership Act (JTPA) The most recent manpower training program is the Job Training Partnership Act (JTPA). This law, enacted in 1982, authorizes a series of employment and training programs for various target groups. The largest program, under Title IIA of the Act, provides block grants to the states for the administration of employment and training services for economically disadvantaged youth, adults, and long-term unemployed persons. The states are responsible for allocating funds, by formula, to cities and counties with populations of 200,000 or more, known as service delivery areas (SDAs). Funds are appropriated on a Program Year (PY) basis, from July 1 through June 30.

Under Title IIA of JTPA, programs are administered in service delivery areas under a public-private partnership arrangement. Locally elected officials appoint Private Industry Councils (PIC) to plan and oversee local programs. The majority of the PIC members represent business and industry. The remaining members represent other sectors of the community, including education, labor, community-based organizations, the Employment Service, and vocational rehabilitation organizations, and economic development agencies.

Services under the Department of Labor's JTPA program are not limited to job training but also include basic skills and remedial education, counseling, and job placement assistance. The goal of the Act is to move the jobless into permanent and unsubsidized, self-sustaining employment. These programs are usually augmented by supportive services such as child care and transportation.

In addition to Title II programs, many homeless may be eligible to participate in an initiative funded from two other sections of the JTPA legislation: those historically offered under Title III, the state administered dislocated worker training initiative that has been replaced by the Economic Dislocation and Worker Adjustment Act of 1988; and Select Title IV initiatives, special programs funded and administered by the federal government. Under Title IV, the two major federally administered efforts geared at getting the homeless back in the mainstream are Jobs for Homeless Veterans and a special initiative conducted under the Jobs Corps.

The Stewart B. McKinney Homeless Assistance Act (1987) amended the Job Training Partnership Act in two ways. It added the homeless to the definition of who are eligible for JTPA programs, in Section 4(8) of the Act; and it changed the requirement for proof of residency under Section 141(E) of JTPA to permit services to individuals who cannot prove that they reside within a service delivery area, if its job training plan permits services to homeless individuals.

The National Commission for Employment Policy (1990) conducted research on the role of JTPA in improving job prospects for the homeless. They found that professional staff of the 55 urban SDAs surveyed did not consider homeless individuals a group for whom they should be providing services. The following reasons were given: (a) not thinking of the homeless as a group who needed job training services, (b) lack of history serving this group, (c) timing of JTPA's implementation with the 1982-83 recession created a large pool of eligible people who were easy to find, (d) lack of money for support services, (e) emphasis on program performance, and (f) requirements for eligibility. Two-thirds of the respondents did not feel as though their job training program was considered to be a primary resource for many of the agencies, shelters, and community-based organizations dealing with the homeless population. Only half of the administrators applied for McKinney funds. Despite SDA and PIC willingness to include homeless people in programs, 15% of the administrators did not actively recruit homeless people, 55% had modest recruiting efforts, and 30% had more extensive recruiting efforts. Two-thirds of the administrators did not offer any services or programs targeted at the homeless population. Administrators who did offer special programs for the homeless felt that a case management approach was necessary if the participant was to succeed. These services included the following:

1. Negotiating a longer period of residence in a shelter than was normally allowed.

2. Developing an agreement with proprietors of motels, single room occupancy hotels, and other low-cost housing

establishments to ensure a stable living arrangement while the client is in training and during the initial period of employment.

3. Working with social services agencies to find temporary or transitional housing for the individual while he/she was in training.

4. Finding the resources to provide assistance with respect to health and personal hygiene issues.

5. Ensuring that the individual is not a substance abuser. Most of the respondents did not predict a significant change in the type or level of service in their local JPTA programs to the homeless population.

Stewart B. McKinney Homelessness Assistance Act

In 1987, in response to the number of homeless people in the United States, Congress enacted the primary legislation guiding federal homeless policy today—The Stewart B. McKinney Homelessness Assistance Act. The McKinney Act allocated 1,338.3 million dollars, in fiscal year 1995, for programs to assist the homeless (National Coalition for the Homeless, 1994). Most of this money was for urgent need programs such as shelter, food, and health care. Fourteen and one-half million dollars went to education and job training. Adult Education for the Homeless was allocated 9.5 million, and Job Training for the Homeless was allocated 5 million. In Fiscal Year, 1995 the Job Training for the Homeless program was terminated. In the fiscal year, 1996 funding for the McKinney programs was cut by 27% and several programs' funding was eliminated including Adult Education for the Homeless. In addition to funding reductions attempts have been make to repeal authorization for the Adult Education for the Homeless program and the Job Training for the Homeless Program (National Coalition for the Homeless, 1997).

Programs that relate to homeless women with children, education, and job training include:

1. The Adult Education for the Homeless program provides assistance to state education agencies so that they can provide a program of literacy training and basic skills remediation for adult homeless individuals.

2. Training for the Homeless Demonstration Program provides funds for job training activities for homeless individuals, including remedial education, job search activities, job counseling, job preparation training, and basic literacy instruction. The funds are available to state and local public agencies, Native American tribes, private nonprofit organizations, and private businesses.

3. Family Support Center Demonstration Projects authorize demonstrations to provide intensive, comprehensive services to homeless families or families at risk of becoming homeless.

4. Supportive Housing Program—Transitional Housing Program provides funds to develop innovative approaches to providing short-term (24 months or less) housing and support services to homeless persons making the transition to independent living. This program is especially targeted to deinstitutionalized individuals with mental disabilities and homeless families with children. States, units of general local government, public housing agencies, and private, nonprofit agencies are eligible for funds.

5. Education for Homeless Children and Youth—State and Local Grants provide funds to state education agencies to develop and implement programs for the education of homeless children.

The Housing and Community Act of 1992 (Public Law 102-50) amends and extends certain laws related to housing and community development. Some McKinney Act sections were mandated to employ or use the volunteer services of homeless individuals and families, to the maximum extent practicable, in programs funded by the following McKinney Act sections: (a) Emergency Shelter Grants, (b) Section 8 assistance for single room occupancy dwellings, (c) Shelter Plus Care, (d) use of FEMA Inventory for transitional housing for the homeless persons and for turnkey housing, and (e) Federal Emergency Management Food and Shelter Programs (local). The homeless volunteer or are employed to rehabilitate or operate facilities assisted under the McKinney Act sections listed above and provide services for the occupants of those facilities.

Adult Education for the Homeless (AHE) Program The 1987 McKinney Act's Adult Education for the Homeless (AHE) Program is a competitive discretionary grant program. The program provides funds to state educational agencies to plan and implement programs of basic and life skills education for homeless adults. The general purposes of the projects are to provide instruction in basic and life skills, to further assist homeless adults through counseling and life planning activities, and to coordinate efforts with other programs serving homeless adults. Within the title of homeless adults, special populations served include the unemployed/underemployed, various minority populations, victims of spousal abuse, veterans, migrant workers, adults with limited English proficiency, developmentally/physically disabled adults, mentally ill adults, the chemically dependent, victims of natural disasters, and others needing temporary or crisis care. Increasingly, projects develop curricula and services to address the growing number of homeless families and single parents with children.

Many projects develop special instructional materials and methods. Basic and life skills are provided in contexts that are most appropriate to the strengths, goals, and experiences of the individual participant and population that the programs serve. All programs include support services such as transportation and child care during class time. There is extensive coordination with other agencies and service providers to ensure the needs of the homeless learners are met. Basic instruction includes basic literacy and computation, critical thinking and problem solving skills, general education diploma (GED) preparation, and English-as-a-second-language (ESL) instruction. Life skills instruction includes such areas as money management; job readiness; health and hygiene; use of community resources; government, law, and citizenship; housing/independent living skills; and parenting skills.

In a report on the fourth year of the Adult Education for the Homeless Program (U.S. Department of Education, 1993a), 90% of the states reported on the performance of their programs. In 78% of the states, almost 2,000 homeless learners made the transition from basic skills instruction to higher education and occupational training. This was considered a critical factor in assuring a long-term transition to self-sufficiency. In 78% of the states, 3,000 learners found or improved their employment opportunities.

Job Training for the Homeless Demonstration Program (JTHDP) The McKinney Act authorized the Department of Labor to plan and implement the Job Training for the Homeless Demonstration

Program. It is administered by the Employment and Training Administration. The supporting goals of JTHDP are:

1. To gain information on how to provide effective employment and training services to homeless individuals, to address the employment-related causes of the homeless, and to address their job training needs.

2. To learn how states, local public agencies, private nonprofit organizations, and private businesses can develop effective systems of coordination to address the causes of homelessness and meet the needs of the homeless. The plans must provide coordination and outreach activities, especially with case managers and care providers; provide in-shelter outreach and assessment; and where practical, pre-employment services and other similar activities that will increase participation in their project.

The job training-related activities include basic skills instruction, remedial education activities, basic literacy instruction, job search activities, job counseling, job preparatory training, and any other activities described in Section 204 of the Job Training Partnership Act (JTPA). Five of the most important activities include institutional skills training, on-the-job training, work experience, follow-up services, and supportive services. A "logic model" was developed to assist in project development. The elements include (a) a sequence of employment and training services followed by intake/assessment, job training, job placement, and retention; (b) a wide range of support services, including housing, specialized assessment, transportation, and child care; and (c) case management as the element that would link the employment and training and supportive services together.

The Job Training for the Homeless Demonstration Program was evaluated by the Department of Labor in 1994. The principle findings included:

1. Employment and training programs can successfully serve a wide spectrum of the homeless. Participants ranged from 14 to 79 years old with 32 the average age. Fifty-one percent of the participants were between 22 and 34 years old. Sixty-five percent were men and 38% were white. One-third did not have a high school diploma or GED. Fifty percent had not been employed in the last 20 or more weeks. Sixty percent had been

homeless for less than four months. The JTHDP participants were somewhat more employable than those in other homeless studies.

2. A small percentage of the United States homeless population is currently served by Department of Labor (DOL) employment and training programs.

3. A wide variety of public and private agencies can successfully establish and operate employment and training programs for homeless persons.

4. Employment and training programs for homeless persons must offer an array of services--including housing services--often requiring linkages with other service providers.

5. Employment and training programs serving homeless individuals require comprehensive assessment and ongoing case management.

6. Employment and training programs need to provide short-term job search/placement services.

7. Long-term follow-up and support was needed.

8. One-third of the homeless participants were likely to secure jobs, and half of those securing jobs were likely to be employed 13 weeks later.

9. Forty percent of the participants upgraded their housing and 25% secured housing.

10. Costs varied across sites depending on the types of participants served and types of training provided.

The report cited the following implications:

1. Access to the program could be enhanced in the following ways. Expand outreach and recruitment practices to include linkages with homeless-serving agencies. Incorporate a housing intervention strategy into the program. Expand the current coordination arrangements. Seek state incentive grant set-asides. Provide additional training to their staff and to their service providers.

2. Encourage programs to use a long-term job retention and housing strategy.

3. Extend the period for tracking outcomes of program participants.

4. Encourage local housing authorities to target homeless participants for transitional and permanent housing opportunities.

5. Provide multi-year grants to successful programs.

PROGRAM AREAS AND COMPONENTS

During the 1960s, 1970s, and 1980s, government programs were created, modified, and expanded to meet the needs of the homeless with some programs addressing the needs of homeless families. Most, if not all, of those programs are based on a model that assumes that training, educating, and providing short-term support services will afford homeless people the abilities to find employment that is adequate to support a household. Leaving aside economic factors such as recessions and the need for job creation, research has indicated that, for the model to be successful for homeless families, all of the following program areas and components may be needed (program areas are in bold print):

1. **Case Management**—Is important in the delivery of services because homeless women face multiple barriers to employment. Participation is needed by agencies in the fields of training, education, counseling, and family services. Case management must be used to ensure that the homeless women receive an appropriate mix of services in an appropriate time frame. Based on needs assessment findings, the case manager works with each client to develop an individual plan of action with short- and long-term goals, to identify barriers to be overcome, to determine the necessary service mix, and to assist the client in communication with service providers.

2. **Needs Assessment**—Is a service plan that is developed for each family upon entry to the program taking into account the unique needs of the family. Subsequent to outreach and intake, and prior to action plan development, each program participant undergoes a complete assessment that includes basic skills

testing, career aptitude testing and evaluation, mental and dental examination, and psychological evaluation.

3. Child-Care—Is considered crucial to success because the clients are women with dependent children.

4. Transportation Assistance—Is important to success among participants because public transportation is frequently inadequate in neighborhoods.

5. On-Site Delivery of Services—There are advantages to on-site delivery of services (for example, the lack or transportation and the reluctance of persons to travel outside of their neighborhoods).

6. Client Participation—Clients need to be consulted about their needs and preferences in the planning and the delivering of services.

7. Commitment and Communication—Of critical importance is commitment and communication among service providers in bringing a variety of resources to bear on the problems of the target group.

8. Health Services—Families need to receive complete medical evaluation and preventative services including pre-natal care for pregnant women and immunizations for children.

9. Educational Enhancement—The women need literacy and basic education programs. The children also need educational support due to lack of basic education and delayed development.

10. Foster Care Prevention—In a transitional setting, the following support systems are necessary for foster care prevention: crisis nursery, intensive family counseling, and crisis intervention.

11. Substance Abuse Treatment—Treatment and counseling must be provided for mothers and children with substance abuse problems.

12. Independent Living Skills—Workshops are needed to address issues of home management skills, parenting, domestic violence, child development, self-esteem, housing maintenance, and budgeting. The workshops help families to develop the independent living skills necessary to retain housing.

13. Employment Training and Placement—Employment training and work experience programs give adults the motivation, knowledge, and experience to move from welfare dependence to employment and self sufficiency. Placement and follow-up assist the women in maintaining stable, decent jobs.

14. Post-Placement Services—Caseworkers visit families for up to one year and offer counseling, client advocacy, and linkages to available community resources (Blank, Collins, & Smith, 1992; Da Costa Nunez, 1994; Institute for Children and Poverty, 1994; Lam, 1989; Liebow, 1993; National Commission on Employment Policy, 1990; New York State Education Department, 1990a; Office of Policy Development and Research, 1995; Office of Vocational and Adult Education, 1992; Rossi, 1994b; U.S. Department of Education, 1993a; U.S. Department of Labor, 1991, 1994).

SUMMARY

Family homelessness is a complex social issue. Its ultimate roots lie in the restructuring of the American economy and the decline in the market demand for unskilled workers (Rossi, 1994b). Poor young men and women, especially minorities have lacked the education and skills that would allow them to find employment that would enable them to establish independent households through marriage. Since the 1980s, women with children have been identified as the fastest growing segment of the homeless population by homeless studies, with homeless families constituting one-third of the homeless population. The typical homeless family as reflected in the literature is a young woman with two or three dependent children, most under the age of six years (Bassuk & Buckner, 1994; DaCosta Nunez, 1994).

One of the causes of homelessness is the failure for marriage formation due to the decline in employment opportunities for minority males. In the 1930s, the unemployment of the time led to the postponement of marriage and childbearing; whereas today, the widespread unemployment has led to the failure of marriages to form, but not childbearing and rearing. In earlier centuries, there were few homeless families. Those that did exist were provided for by their family. Today, these families are themselves impoverished with limited resources to help their family members. Domestic and child abuse has also increased, forcing many women and children out of intolerable living situations.

The lack of sufficient income and stagnation and loss of low income housing stock has resulted in poor families competing for the low income rental stock that is available and paying more of their income toward housing. Single parents face additional financial and emotional challenges to handle full-time work and the demands of being a sole parent. The sole responsibility of dependent children places an individual at a disadvantage in the work force. Women are also more likely to face various forms of gender-based discrimination in the work force. The final result has been an increase of precariously housed women with children. These women lack the financial resources and social ties to support their families.

One of the long-term solutions for homelessness is the improvement of employment opportunities for all Americans, but especially groups experiencing high levels of unemployment and withdrawal from the work force. Homeless women with children are one of these groups. Education and job training is needed that will prepare the women for jobs in the restructured economy. These jobs would help the women become self sufficient. Homeless women with children need a supportive environment that provides a stable living environment and supportive services to reach self sufficiency. Specific support services include health care, drug and alcohol rehabilitation, child care, socialization, family therapy, literacy and basic education, home management and parenting education, job training and placement, and follow-up when the women find housing and employment.

CHAPTER 3

Research Methods

INTRODUCTION

The main purpose of the study was to develop a transitional program framework that can assist homeless women with children to become self-sufficient. In order to create this framework, the study identified current program areas and components in transitional programs for homeless women with children, including education and employment training components, and determined which program areas and components of current programs have a relationship to those programs with successful outcomes.

The approach used in this study was descriptive survey research. The descriptive survey research involved systematic data collection in order to address questions concerning characteristics of the current programs and participants, current program areas and components including educational and employment training; importance of the program areas and components; and program outcomes. The mailed questionnaire is one of the most commonly used survey methods because it is inexpensive, can be self-administered and is anonymous. Problems with this method of research include low response rates and lack of validation; for example, when questions are not understood or answered correctly by the intended respondent. In spite of the limitations, the mailed questionnaire offers the best method to collect data from a diverse and widely dispersed population. The methodology for this research project was designed to accomplish the three goals of the study:

1. To identify, characterize, and analyze the current transitional programs for homeless women with children.

2. To determine the current program areas and components, perceived program area and component importance, and program outcomes.

3. To determine which program demographics, programs areas, and components are related to successful program outcomes and are important in effective transitional programs.

POPULATION

The population under study was transitional shelter/housing programs for homeless women with children in the 29 cities in the continental United States that participated in the 1994 U.S. Conference of Mayors' annual 30-city survey, which was used to determine the status of hunger and homelessness in America's cities. The U.S. Conference of Mayor's annual report identified the following information and estimates from each city:

1. The demand for emergency food assistance and emergency shelter and the capacity of local agencies to meet the demand.

2. The causes of hunger and homelessness and the demographics of the populations experiencing these problems.

3. Exemplary programs or efforts in the cities to respond to hunger and homelessness.

4. The availability of affordable housing for low income people.

5. The outlook for the future.

6. The most important federal actions that need to be taken to prevent and respond to homelessness.

These annual studies have not only included findings about hunger, homelessness, and housing; they also provide a comparative overview of all preceding years. The most current study, December, 1994, gives a 10-year comparison of data. The data for the study are from community-based provider and government agencies. These data are supplemented with data on population, poverty, and unemployment available from the U.S. Bureau of the Census and the U.S. Bureau of Labor Statistics. These supportive data offer the researcher background and a broad basis for comparison.

In order to identify transitional shelters and housing programs, the researcher contacted by telephone the Assistant Executive Director at the U.S. Conference of Mayors and requested a list of contact persons in the cities that participated in the 1994 U.S. Conference of Mayors' annual survey on the status of hunger and homelessness in America's cities. The cities included Alexandria, VA; Boston, MA; Charleston, SC; Charlotte, NC; Chicago, IL; Cleveland, OH, Denver, CO; Detroit, MI; Kansas City, MO; Los Angeles, CA; Louisville, KY; Miami, FL; Minneapolis, MN; Nashville, TN; New Orleans, LA; New York City, NY; Norfolk, VA; Philadelphia, PA; Portland, OR; Providence, RI; Saint Louis, MO; Saint Paul, MN; Salt Lake City, UT; San Antonio, TX; San Diego, CA; San Francisco, CA; Santa Monica, CA; Seattle WA; and Trenton, NJ.

Next, the researcher telephoned each city's survey contact person and requested a list of transitional shelter/housing programs in their city that serve homeless women with children. A phone call was made to all identified transitional shelters/housing programs to determine the correct program address, to determine if the program was transitional, to identify the program director, and to determine if the program director would be willing to participate in the survey. A final list of 116 transitional shelters/housing programs were identified in the cities. The list of transitional shelters/housing programs was placed in a database that included the program's name, director's name, program's address, and program's telephone number. All of the 116 identified transitional shelter/housing programs were surveyed.

RESEARCH DESIGN

An initial review of literature was conducted to determine program profiles; client profiles; program outcomes; and program areas and components. From this information a proposed survey instrument was developed. The questionnaire consisted of closed or structured questions. The questions were followed by choices or rating scales. The advantages to this type of question is that they are usually easy and quick to answer and involve little writing. In addition, analysis is straight-forward. The disadvantages are that the responses are provided by the researcher and there is a loss of spontaneity on the part of the respondent.

An expert panel reviewed the proposed survey instrument. The expert panel consisted of six identified practitioners and experts in homelessness, education, employment training, and transitional shelter/housing programs. These persons included a representative from the U. S. Department of Housing and Urban Development's (HUD) Office of Special Needs and Assistance Programs, job training practitioners, Massachusetts Cooperative Extension Nutrition and Family Development professionals, and transitional shelter/housing program directors. A cover letter and proposed survey instrument was sent on July 14, 1995 to those identified experts. A copy of the cover letter is included in Appendix B. The expert panel members were asked to comment on the following:

1. Clarity and appropriateness of directions and title.

2. Completeness of the content of program components, program outcomes, and program and client profile questions. They were asked to note any program components, program outcomes, program profile questions, or client profile questions that should be added or deleted.

3. Clarity of statements.

4. Appropriateness of scales and concepts to accomplish the purpose of the instrument.

5. Organization of the survey. If the layout was a problem, what would they suggest?

6. Length of the instrument.

The panel members responded by August 1, 1995. The survey instrument was revised based on their comments.

To test the revised survey instrument and determine if it would solicit adequate replies, a pilot test was conducted at transitional shelter/housing programs in six programs in Connecticut and Massachusetts, excluding Boston programs. A list of shelters was obtained from the Massachusetts and Connecticut Coalitions for the Homeless. Transitional shelter directors in western Massachusetts and Connecticut were contacted by phone and asked to participate in the pilot test of the survey instrument. On September 18, 1995, a cover letter and copy of the pilot test survey was sent to the six transitional shelter directors. A copy of the cover letter is included in Appendix C. Four of the six programs responded by October 4, 1995. The surveys were evaluated for length of time to complete, question content, and clarity of directions and statements. These steps were used to insure the validity of the survey instrument In all cases, the respondents reported that each of the questions were clear and valid to the purpose of the study. The pilot test respondents' comments did not suggest any changes to the survey instrument. After evaluation of the pilot study, the final survey instrument was prepared, which appears in Appendix E.

The final survey instrument was mailed to 116 identified transitional shelter/housing program directors. To increase the return rate, the researcher included a letter of explanation, personally signed by the researcher, with each initial site-coded survey and a stamped pre-addressed envelope. A copy of the cover letter is included in Appendix D. The first mailing was sent out on October 23, 1995. The cutoff date for responses was November 13, 1995. No money or any item of monetary value was offered as compensation or reward to entice a response to this study. Each cover letter offered a summary of the data collected on the condition the request was received in a letter separate from the questionnaire in order not to compromise the anonymity of the respondent. This offer was not dependent on the return of the survey. Fifty-four requests were received for a summary of the data. On November 10, 1995, a reminder postcard was sent to each program director in the database. A copy is included in Appendix F. A total of 71 surveys were received by the cutoff date. These 71 surveys represented a 61 percent response rate for the initial mailing. The researcher followed-up with a telephone call to non-respondents to increase the response rate. A second mailing was sent to those who had misplaced their original survey. This resulted in the return of seven additional surveys bringing the total surveys returned to 78. These late surveys increased the response rate to 67 percent. A one-way ANOVA was used to test for potential differences between the means of the on-time surveys and the late surveys. The test results suggested that the late surveys could be combined with the on-time surveys.

ANALYSIS OF DATA

Appropriate statistical information was analyzed using *Statistical Program for the Social Sciences (SPSS) for Windows, Release 6.0* software. *SPSS* software was chosen for the statistical analysis due to its programming flexibility and simplicity of use.

Data from the received questionnaires were reviewed, coded, and entered into the SPSS for Windows computer database. The data were analyzed in several ways. The level of significance used to decide whether to accept or reject the null hypothesis (alpha level) was set *a priori* at the probability value of .10 (Borg & Gall, 1989). Basic descriptive statistics were produced, including frequencies, percentages, means, and correlations. These statistics determined how the total sample distributed itself on the various response alternatives such as the current components used in the programs, where provided, and who provides the service; the importance of various program components in a transitional program; and characteristics of the programs and participants they serve. Basic descriptive statistical procedures, analysis of variance, and other necessary tests were conducted on variables to determine relationships between certain variables such as:

1. Current program areas and components/ program outcomes;

2. Type of program/current program areas and components;

3. Type of program/ program outcomes;

4. Size of program (number of individual family living units)/current program areas and components;

5. Size of program (number of individual family living units)/ program outcomes;

6. Length of program/program outcomes; and

7. Length of program/current program areas and components.

Chi-square was the statistical technique used to test the hypothesis that the two variables of the crosstabulation were independent of each other. Chi-square is a nonparametric statistical test used to determine the statistical significance of the differences between the observed frequencies and those frequencies that would be expected from normative data. Chi-square was used on all crosstabulations.

A one-way analysis of variance (ANOVA) was the statistical technique used to evaluate whether the groups differed significantly among themselves on the variables being studied. ANOVA examines variability of the observations within each group as well as the variability between the groups. Based on these two estimates of variability, conclusions about the population means could be drawn. The data were tested to see if its variability (as measured by its variance) was random, or part of the variance was the result of systematic differences between samples. In this study, one-way ANOVA was used to test the hypothesis that the mean of the late surveys was equal to the on-time surveys. The second analysis was the null hypothesis that the mean number of program components in each program area were equal in all outcome levels.

A Scheffe´ test was done on ANOVA results where the F ratio was statistically significant. The Scheffe´ test is a special t-test which takes into account that a researcher may find significant results because many comparisons were made on the same data (Borg & Gall, 1989). No other statistical technique was found appropriate.

LIMITATIONS OF THE STUDY

There was no comprehensive mailing list of transitional homeless shelters/housing programs available due to the decentralization of the shelter system. Shelters may be reluctant to give information on their address, especially if the shelter includes battered women. The data were self-reported by program directors and no secondary sources (for example, review of client records) were consulted to corroborate responses. Some program directors may have consulted detailed records to provide responses, whereas others may have relied on memory, introducing a possible source of inconsistency and bias. Only aggregate data on clients were collected, not personal, or household level data. Those data will not permit a detailed analysis of individual household characteristics, history, or outcomes. This limits the extent to which program impact can be assessed.

SUMMARY

A descriptive research methodology was used for data collection. A survey questionnaire was sent to program directors of transitional shelter/housing programs for homeless women with children in the 29 continental United States cities that participated in the 1994 U.S. Conference of Mayors' annual 30-city survey. The descriptive survey research involved systematic data collection in order to address questions concerning characteristics of the programs and participants; current program areas and components, including education and employment training components; importance of the program areas and components; and program outcomes. Data from the received questionnaires were reviewed, coded, and entered into the SPSS for Windows computer database. The data were analyzed in several ways. Basic descriptive statistical procedures, analysis of variance, and other necessary tests were conducted on variables to determine relationships between certain variables.

Presentation and Interpretation of Data

RESEARCH METHODS

Chapter 4 is devoted to reporting the results of the study. The data were obtained from questionnaires returned by directors of transitional programs that serve homeless women with children. The main purpose of this study was to develop a transitional program framework that can assist homeless women with children to become self-sufficient. In order to create this framework; this study identified current program areas and components in transitional programs for homeless women with children, including education and employment training components; and determined which program areas and components of current programs have a relationship to programs with successful outcomes.

The three goals of this study and respective research questions were:

Goal 1: To identify, characterize, and analyze the current transitional programs for homeless women with children.

1. What are the profiles of the transitional programs for homeless women with children?

2. What are the profiles of transitional program participants?

Goal 2: To determine the current program areas and components, perceived program area and component importance, and program outcomes.

3. What are the program areas and components in current transitional programs?

4. Where are the program areas and components provided?

5. Who provides the program area and components?

6. What is the perceived importance of each program areas and component in transitional programs?

7. What are the current programs' outcomes?

Goal 3: To determine which program demographics, program areas and components are related to successful program outcomes and are important in effective transitional programs.

8. What are the demographics of programs with successful outcomes?

9. Which program areas and components are present in programs with successful outcomes?

10. Which program demographics, program areas, and components are important in an effective transitional program framework?

Goal 1: Identification, Characterization, and Analysis of Current Transitional Programs for Homeless Women With Children

A total of 71 surveys were returned by the cutoff date. After a reminder phone call, seven more survey instruments were returned increasing the total returned surveys to 78. A one-way ANOVA was used to test for potential differences between the means of the on-time surveys and the late surveys. No difference was found in the means at the .05 level of significance. Consequently the null hypotheses was rejected with 95% confidence. In other words, the test results suggested that the late surveys could be combined with the on-time surveys. The use of valid observations/percentage in the data presentation represents the actual number or percentage of responses for that particular question.

The surveys were coded for the transitional program's geographical location. The transitional program locations were determined as follows:

East—Alexandria, VA; Boston, MA; Charleston, SC; Charlotte, NC; Miami, FL; Nashville TN; New Orleans, LA; New York City, NY; Norfolk, VA; Philadelphia, PA; Providence, RI; Trenton, NJ;

Mid-West—Chicago, IL; Detroit, MI, Kansas City, MO; Louisville, KY; Minneapolis, MN; St. Louis, MO; Saint Paul, MN; San Antonio, TX;

West—Denver, CO; Los Angeles, CA; Portland, OR; Salt Lake City, UT; San Diego, CA; San Francisco, CA; Santa Monica CA; Seattle WA.

Each city was represented in the sample. The sample was uniformly distributed in all geographical locations as shown in Table 4.1.

Table 4.1: Geographical Locations of Responding Transitional Programs

Location	Number of Respondents	Percentage of Programs
East	25	32.0
Midwest	29	37.2
West	24	30.8
Total	78	100.0

Note. Number of valid observations = 78. Missing responses = 0

Of the 78 valid cases, 96.2 % of the surveyed programs provided services for homeless women with children and 3.8% did not provide services for homeless women with children; therefore, there were 75 valid cases.

Question 1: What are the profiles of the transitional programs?

The five program description categories are presented in Table 4.2. The directors described 57.3 % of the programs as transitional housing and 26.7 % as transitional shelters. None of the responding programs were domestic violence shelters.

Table 4.2: Program Directors' Descriptions of Their Programs

Program Description	Number of Programs	Valid Percentage
Transitional Shelter	20	26.7
Emergency and Transitional Shelter	9	12.0
Transitional Housing	43	57.3
Domestic Violence Shelter	0	00.0
Other	3	4.0
Total	75	100.0

Note. Number of valid observations = 75. Missing responses = 3.

The programs are categorized by the number of individual family living units. Approximately 56% of the programs had 5-15 units. Of those remaining, 18.7 % had 25 or more units.

Table 4.3: Number of Individual Family Living Units in Programs

Number of Individual Family Living Units	Number of Programs	Valid Percentage
Less than 5	8	10.7
5-10	28	37.3
11-15	13	17.3
16-20	7	9.3
21-25	5	6.7
Over 25	14	18.7
Total	75	100.0

Note. Number of valid observations = 75. Missing responses = 3

The data shown in Table 4.4 indicate that, for more than one-third of the programs, the program length was 19-24 months. The length category with the next highest percentage of programs (26.7%) was 1-6 months. Of the programs studied, 96% met the guidelines of the Supportive Housing Program, which specifies that funds may be used in transitional housing designed to enable homeless persons and families to move to permanent housing within a 24-month period.

Table 4.4: Length of Program

Program Length	Number of Programs	Valid Percentage
1-6 Months	20	26.7
7-12 Months	13	17.3
13-18 Months	11	14.7
19-24 Months	28	37.3
Over 24 Months	3	4.0
Total	75	100.0

Note. Number of valid observations = 75. Missing responses = 3

The linkages between programs and agencies/organizations are detailed in Table 4.5. Over 92% of the programs reported connections to housing, welfare, or social service agencies. Over 80% of the programs reported links with employment, mental health, and community non-profit service providers. At least 68% of the programs had linkages with educational institutions and employment training programs. Forty-nine percent of the programs had linkages with the business community.

The funding sources for programs are presented in Tables 4.6 a and b. The scale used for responses reported in Table 4.6 is as follows: 1 = Most Important Funding Source; 2 = Important Funding Source; 3 = Less Important Funding Source; and 4 = Not a Funding Source. The Supportive Housing Program (SHP)/Transitional Housing Program was ranked the most important funding source by 48.5% of the programs and an important source by 19.1% of the programs, whereas 32.4% of the programs reported it was not a source of funds. The SHP/Transitional Housing Program is federally funded and awards its monies on the basis of grant applications. Other important sources of funding include private individuals and organizations, religious groups, and state and local governments.

Table 4.5: Agencies and Other Organizations That Have Linkages With the Programs

Linking Agencies/Organizations	Number of Programs	Percentage of Programs
Welfare Agencies	70.0	93.3
Social Service Agencies	70.0	93.3
Housing Providers	69.0	92.0
Job Service	62.0	82.7
Mental Health Organizations	62.0	82.7
Community Advocates	60.0	80.0
Job Training Providers/Vocational Centers	59.0	84.3
Non-Profit/Religious Organizations	59.0	78.7
Non-Profit/Secular Organizations	59.0	78.7
Educational Institutions/Providers	57.0	76.0
Welfare to Work Programs	51.0	68.0
Businesses	39.0	52.0
JTPA Private Industry Council	37.0	49.3
State Cooperative Extension	25.0	33.3
Other Linkages	7.0	9.3

Note. Number of valid observations = 75. Missing responses = 3. Columns do not total 100% because of multiple responses.

Table 4.6: Source of Funding for Programs

a. Sources of Funding for Programs Ranked by Order of Importance

Funding Sources	Mean	SD	*n* (N = 78)
SHP/Transitional Housing Program	2.16	1.33	68
Individual Contributions	2.41	1.20	68
Local Government Funds	2.62	1.27	71
Foundations	2.71	1.15	68
State Government Funds	2.76	1.28	68
Private Sector Organization	2.85	1.10	68
Non-Profit/Religious	2.94	1.12	68
United Way	3.04	1.03	68
Community Service Block Grant	3.19	1.07	68
Other Federal Government Program	3.43	1.03	68
Non-Profit Organization	3.47	.80	68
Title IIA of JTPA	3.82	.52	68
Federal Anti-Drug Funds	3.96	.21	68
Carl D. Perkins Vocational Ed Act	3.97	.17	68

Note. Differences between valid *n* and *N* caused by missing responses. Scale for this question was: 1 = Most Important Funding Source; 2 = Important Funding Source; 3 = Less Important Funding Source; 4 = Not a Funding Source. SHP(Supportive Housing Program). JTPA (Job Training Partnership Act).

b. Distribution by Importance of Funding Sources for Programs

	Importance Percentage Distribution			
	Most Important	Important	Less Important	Not a Funding Source
SHP/Transitional Housing Program	48.5	19.1		32.4
Individual Contributions	32.4	20.5	20.6	26.5
Local Government Funds	28.2	21.1	11.3	39.4
Foundations	17.6	30.9	14.7	36.8
State Government Funds	25.0	20.5	7.4	47.1
Private Sector Organization	13.3	27.9	19.1	39.7
Non-Profit/Religious	13.2	25.0	16.2	45.6
United Way	5.9	32.4	13.2	48.5
Community Service Block Grant	7.4	26.5	5.8	60.3
Other Federal Government Program	10.3	8.8	8.8	72.1
Non-Profit Organization	2.9	10.3	23.5	63.2
Title IIA of JTPA	5.9		5.9	88.2
Federal Anti-Drug Funds			4.4	95.6
Carl D. Perkins Vocational Ed Act			2.9	97.1

Question 2: What are the profiles of transitional program participants?

The number of participants by type in the responding programs are shown in Table 4.7. The vast majority of participants were women with children. This finding is consistent with the U.S. Conference of Mayors' Survey (1994), which found that 78% of homeless families were headed by a single parent.

Table 4.7: Types and Number of Participants in Responding Programs

Type of Participant	Number	Percentage of Total	*n* (*N* = 78)
Women with Children	1,970	81.2	69
Single Men	168	6.6	67
Single Women	139	5.7	66
Intact Families	132	5.4	65
Men with Children	27	1.1	65
Total	2,428	100.0	

Note. Differences between valid *n* and *N* are caused by missing responses.

As shown in Table 4.8, women between the ages of 20 and 34 represented 74.6% of the women with children in the programs. Women 35 years and older represented 17.6% of the women with children in the programs. Women 19 years old or younger represented 7.8% of the women with children in the programs.

Studies by the Institute of Medicine (1988), Lam (1987), DaCosta Nunez (1994), Rossi (1989a), Wright and Lam (1987), Wright (1989), Wright and Weber (1987) found that the "new homeless" are younger, in their early 20s. Bassuk et al. (1986) and McChesney (1987) found that homeless women with children tended to be in their late 20s. The findings of this study confirm this age distribution.

The racial status of women with children in the responding programs is reported in Table 4.9. Black women with children made up 65.1% of the participants. Hispanic women with children made up 20.7% of the participants. White women with children made up 11.5% of the participants. These findings are similar to Burt's (1992) findings that women with children are more likely than any other homeless group to be a member of a minority group.

Table 4.8: Ages of Women with Children in Responding Programs

Age Category	Number	Percent of Total	n ($N = 78$)
Under 15 Years Old	24	1.3	63
15-19 Years Old	116	6.5	63
20-24 Years Old	434	24.0	61
25-29 Years Old	524	29.0	62
30-34 Years Old	390	21.6	62
35-39 Years Old	188	10.4	62
Over 40 Years Old	130	7.2	61
Total	1,806	100.0	

Note. Differences between valid n and N are caused by missing responses.

Table 4.9: Race of Women With Children in Responding Programs

Race	Number	Percentage of Total
White	155	11.5
Black	884	65.2
Hispanic	280	20.7
Asian	16	1.2
North American Indian	9	.7
Other	9	.7
Total	1,353	100.0

Note. Number of valid observations = 60. Missing responses = 18.

The marital status of women with children in the responding programs is categorized in Table 4.10. Most of the women (72.2%) were single. Only 1.2% were widowed. The other participants were either married (8.4%), separated (8.6%), or divorced (9.5%).

Table 4.10: Marital Status of Women With Children in Responding Programs

Marital Status	Number	Percentage of Total	*n* (N = 78)
Single	858	72.2	58
Married	99	8.4	57
Separated	102	8.7	57
Divorced	113	9.5	58
Widowed	14	1.2	56
Total	1,178	100.0	

Note. Differences between valid *n* and *N* are caused by missing responses.

The homeless women in the study usually had two to three children. This finding is identical to those of Burt (1992), Bassuk and Buckner (1994), Bassuk et al. (1986), DaCosta Nunez (1994), Jencks (1994), and Lam (1987). The age distribution of children in the responding programs is presented in Table 4.11. Children five years or younger made up 58.8% of the children in the programs. Children ages 6-12 made up 29.1% of the children in the programs. Only 12.1% of the children in the programs were 12-18 years old. Previous studies by Bassuk and Buckner (1994) and DaCosta Nunez (1994) have found that most of the children of homeless women are under the age of six.

Table 4.11: Age of Children in Responding Programs

Age Category	Number	Percentage of Total	*n* (N = 78)
2 or Younger	731	29.5	64
3-5 Years	725	29.3	64
6-12 Years	719	29.1	64
12-18 Years	300	12.1	63
Total	2,475	100.0	

Note. Differences between valid *n* and *N* are caused by missing responses.

The reasons for participants homelessness and the frequency of their reasons are shown in Tables 4.12 a and b. Participants were asked to rate each factor on the following scale: 1 = Most Frequent Factor; 2 = More Frequent Factor; 3 = Frequent Factor; 4 = Less Frequent Factor; and 5 = Not a Factor. Reasons for homelessness can be broken down into tiers. The tier percentages are derived by collapsing the percentages for the most frequent, more frequent, and frequent cause of homelessness as indicated by the responding program directors. The top tier was physical abuse at 90.2 %. This reason has been cited by Bassuk et al. (1986), DaCosta Nunez (1994), Lam (1987), and Rossi (1989a; 1994b). The second tier concerned issues of housing, such as lack of affordable housing (88.7%) or eviction (87.3%). The National Coalition for the Homeless (1994) noted that these issues face policy makers in respect to family homelessness. The third tier involved the following personal or health issues: family threw them out—81.7%; divorce or termination of personal relationship—75.6%; chronic drug use—66.1%; and chronic alcohol use—64.8%. This finding corresponds to that of Golden (1992), Jencks (1994), Lam (1987), and Liebow (1993). The fourth tier concerned loss or lack of employment at 53.5%. Lam (1987) and Salerno, Hopper, and Baxter (1984) cite a decline in employment opportunities as a reason for homelessness. They also note that homeless women with children face additional employment issues. The next most frequent reasons according to the program directors were releases from substance abuse treatment (49.3%) and mental illness (44.1%). These also have been frequently cited reason in studies by Burt (1992), Institute of Medicine (1988), Lam (1987), Rossi (1989b; 1994b), Wright (1989), Wright and Weber (1987).

The levels of education attained by participants in the responding programs are presented in Table 4.13. The majority of the participants (59.3%) failed to graduate from a high school or a vocational technical school. This finding is similar to that of Bassuk et al. (1986) and McChesney (1987). Graduates of high school and vocational technical schools made up 32.5% of the participants. Only 8.2% of the participants were involved in education beyond these levels.

The employment status of participants before entering the program is reported in Table 4.14. The majority (65.7%) of the participants were either unemployed or had never been employed. Less than half of that number (30.2%) had been employed full-time, part-time, or sporadically. Burt and Cohen (1989) found that 37% of homeless

Table 4.12: Reasons for Participants' Homelessness

a. Frequent Reasons Cited for Participants' Homelessness

Reason For Homelessness	Rated Value of 3 or Less	Mean	SD	n (N = 78)
Physical Abuse	90.2	2.00	1.10	72
Lack of Affordable Housing	88.7	2.00	1.20	71
Evicted From Home	87.3	2.24	1.19	71
Family Threw Them Out	81.7	2.52	1.17	71
Divorce or Termination of Personal Relationship	75.6	2.56	1.35	70
Chronic Drug Use	66.1	2.92	1.37	71
Chronic Alcohol Use	64.8	3.06	1.24	71
Lost Job/Lack of Employment Opportunities	53.5	3.34	1.17	71
Releases From Substance Abuse Treatment	49.3	3.41	1.15	71
Mental Illness	44.1	3.71	1.02	70
Housing Condemned	23.7	3.94	.98	72
Termination of Public Assistance	22.5	4.00	.91	71
Personal or Family Illness	25.7	4.04	.89	70
Runaway/Transient	25.3	4.10	.99	71
Relocated for Improved Job Market	16.9	4.23	.88	71
Released from Prison	9.8	4.31	.77	71
Physical Disability	11.4	4.37	.73	70
Released from a Mental Health Institution	9.8	4.45	.75	71

Note. Scale for this question was: 1 = Most Frequent Factor; 2 = More Frequent Factor; 3 = Frequent Factor; 4 = Less Frequent Factor; 5 = Not a Factor. Differences between valid n and N are caused by missing responses.

b. Distribution of Reasons for Participants' Homelessness

Reason	Reason Percentage Distribution				
	Most Frequent	More Frequent	Less Frequent	Frequent	Not A Factor
Physical Abuse	44.4	23.6	22.2	6.9	2.8
Lack of Affordable Housing	47.9	21.1	19.7	5.6	5.6
Evicted From Home	31.0	35.2	21.1	4.2	8.5
Family Threw Them Out	19.7	35.2	26.8	9.9	8.5
Divorce or Termination of Personal Relationship	27.1	27.1	21.4	11.4	12.9
Chronic Drug Use	18.3	23.9	23.9	15.5	18.3
Chronic Alcohol Use	12.7	19.7	32.4	19.7	15.5
Last Job/Lack of Employment Opportunities	7.0	16.9	29.6	28.2	18.3
Releases From Substance Abuse Treatment	7.0	14.1	28.2	32.4	18.3
Mental Illness	2.9	7.1	31.4	32.9	25.7
Housing Condemned	4.2	2.8	16.7	47.2	29.2
Termination of Public Assistance	1.4	5.6	15.5	46.5	31.0
Personal or Family Illness		5.7	20.0	38.6	35.7
Runaway/Transient	1.4	5.6	18.3	31.0	43.7
Relocated for Improved Job Market	1.4	2.8	12.7	38.0	45.1
Released from Prison		4.2	5.6	45.1	45.1
Physical Disability		1.4	10.0	38.6	50.0
Released from a Mental Health Institution		2.8	7.0	32.4	57.7

Table 4.13: Educational Level of Participants

Educational Level	Number of Participants	Percentage of Total
Some High School	617	45.8
High School Graduate	393	29.2
Some College	93	6.9
Grade School Education	90	6.7
Some Vocational/Technical Education	91	6.8
Vocational/Technical School Graduate	44	3.3
College Degree	15	1.1
Graduate School	3	.2
Total	1,346	100.0

Note. Number of valid observations = 61. Missing responses = 17.

women with children had not worked steadily for four years or more. They also found that 35% of homeless women with children had held a steady job with in the last year. Burt (1992), DaCosta Nunez (1994), and Rossi (1989a) found that the new homeless are more likely to be unemployed.

Table 4.14: Participants' Employment Status Before Entering the Program

Employment Status	Number of Participants	Percentage of Total
Unemployed and Not Looking for Work	468	34.4
Never Employed	247	18.4
Employed Sporadically	216	16.7
Unemployed and Looking For Work	173	12.9
Employed Part-time	97	7.2
Employed Full-time	85	6.3
Other	35	2.6
Disabled and Incapable of Being Employed	21	1.5
Total	1,342	100.0

Note. The number of valid observations = 61. Missing responses = 17

The program directors' assessments of the employability of the participants are shown in Table 4.15. The program directors judged that 76.7% of the participants were probably or definitely employable, while 23.3% were probably or definitely not employable.

Table 4.15: Directors' Assessment of Participants' Employability

Employment Assessment	Number of Participants	Percentage of Total
Probably Employable	810	44.3
Definitely Employable	592	32.4
Probably Not Employable	255	14.0
Definitely Not Employable	178	9.3
Total	1,827	100.0

Note. Number of valid observations = 63. Missing responses = 15

The reasons for participant unemployment are reported in Tables 4.16 a and b. Program directors were asked to rate each reason on the following scale: 1 = Most Accountable; 2 = More Accountable; 3 = Accountable; 4 = Less Accountable; and 5 = Not Accountable. Reasons for participants unemployment can be broken down into tiers. The tier percentages are derived by collapsing the percentages for the most accountable, more accountable, and accountable reason for unemployment as indicated by the program directors. The top tier consisted of lack of competitive employment skills (97.3%), lack of education (94.2%), and lack of child care (91.6%). The second tier reasons were lack of interpersonal skills at 82.5% and communication problems at 82.2%. The third tier included lack of employment opportunities (76.7%) and lack of transportation (69.0%). The fourth tier involved issues of health and hygiene: drug abuse—57.9%; alcohol abuse—54.9%; lack of grooming—46.1%; and mental and psychiatric impairment—45.7%. A review of the literature revealed that most researchers failed to study the reasons for unemployment directly; however, Lam (1987) found that 20% of homeless women were not employable because of the lack of job skills and education.

Table 4.16: Reasons for the Unemployment of Participants

a. Reasons for Participants' Unemployment

Reasons for Unemployment	Rated Value of 3 or less	Mean	SD	n (N = 78)
Lack of Competitive Employment Skills	97.3	1.58	.87	71
Lack of Education	94.2	1.77	.91	69
Lack of Child Care	91.6	1.97	1.16	71
Lack of Interpersonal Skills	82.5	2.54	1.15	69
Lack of Employment Opportunities	76.7	2.61	1.32	69
Communication Problems	82.2	2.67	1.22	69
Lack of Transportation	69.0	2.80	1.19	71
Drug Abuse	57.9	3.07	1.32	69
Alcohol Abuse	54.9	3.19	1.28	69
Mental and Psychiatric Impairment	45.7	3.46	1.27	70
Lack of Grooming	46.1	3.54	1.09	65
Discharge from an Institution	26.0	4.07	1.24	69
Physical Disability	14.4	4.17	1.24	69
Too Young	13.8	4.37	.89	65

Note. Scale for this question: 1 = Most Accountable; 2 = More Accountable; 3 = Accountable; 4 = Less Accountable; 5 = Not Accountable. Differences between valid n and N are caused by missing responses.

b. Distributions of Reasons for Participants' Unemployment

	Accountability Percentage Distribution				
Reasons for Unemployment	Most Accountable	More Accountable	Accountable	Less Accountable	Not Accountable
Lack of Competitive Employment Skills	59.1	29.6	8.5		2.8
Lack of Education	49.3	30.4	14.5	5.8	
Lack of Child Care	45.1	28.2	18.3	1.4	7.0
Lack of Employment Opportunities	27.5	18.8	30.5	11.6	11.6
Communication Problems	17.3	29.0	31.9	11.6	10.2
Lack of Transportation	14.1	31.0	23.9	22.5	8.5
Drug Abuse	13.0	23.2	21.7	26.2	15.9
Lack of Interpersonal Skills	17.5	37.7	27.5	8.6	8.7
Alcohol Abuse	8.7	24.7	21.7	27.5	17.4
Mental and Psychiatric Impairment	10.0	10.0	25.7	31.4	22.9
Lack of Grooming	3.0	12.4	30.8	33.8	20.0
Discharge from an Institution	5.7	5.8	14.5	21.7	52.3
Physical Disability	7.2	2.9	4.3	33.3	52.3
Too Young	1.5	3.2	9.2	29.2	56.9

Goal 2: Current Program Areas and Components, Program Area and Component Importance, and Program Outcomes

Question 3: What are the program areas and components in current transitional programs?

The nine program areas and their respective components of transitional programs for homeless women with children are presented in Table 4.17. Program areas and components used in this study were compiled from the following sources: studies by Burt and Cohen (1989), DaCosta Nunez, (1994), Institute for Children and Poverty (1994), Lam (1987), and Rossi (1989a; 1994b); United States government reports from the Department of Education (1993a), Department of Housing and Urban Development (1995), Department of Labor (1991, 1994); the New York State Education Department (1990); and a review of the author's proposed components by an expert panel.

All programs provided Family and Independent Living Skills Education. Within this area, at least 80% of the programs provided all of the components with the exception of stress management education and time management education.

All programs provided Family Health and Preservation components. Within this area, at least 83% of the programs provided all of the components with the exception of mentoring/peer support, substance abuse treatment, foster care prevention, and family reunification.

All programs provided Support Services. Within this area, at least 82% of the programs provided all of the components with the exception of case worker follow-up—education, case worker follow-up—employment, transportation assistance, legal assistance, and clothing/work equipment assistance.

Case Management was provided by 98.7% of the programs. Within this area, at least 94% of the programs provided all of the components.

Permanent Housing Assistance was provided by 98.7% of the programs. Within this area, at least 81% of the programs provided all of the components.

Children's Programs were provided by 95.9% of the programs. Within this area, at least 82% of the programs provided all the components with the exception of activities during parent meetings and art/play therapy.

Table 4.17: Program Areas and Components in Current Transitional Programs

Program Areas and Components	*n* (*N* = 78)	Number of Programs	Percentage of Programs
Family and Independent Living Skills Education	**75**	**75**	**100.00**
Use of Community Resources Education	74	73	98.6
Parenting Education	73	72	98.6
Budget and Money Management Education	73	72	97.3
Self Esteem, Motivation, and Attitude Development	75	72	96.0
Housing and Independent Living Education	74	68	91.9
HIV/STD Awareness	73	65	89.0
Child Abuse Awareness Education	73	64	87.7
Nutrition Education	74	64	86.5
Child Development, and Behavior Management Education	74	67	85.2
Health and Hygiene Education	74	63	85.1
Legal Issues Education	74	63	85.1
Domestic Violence Awareness	74	62	83.8
Credit and Debt Management Education	73	59	80.8
Stress Management Education	74	57	77.0
Time Management Education	73	56	76.7

Table 4.17 (continued)

Program Areas and Components	n (N = 78)	Number of Programs	Percentage of Programs
Family Health and Preservation	**75**	**75**	**100.0**
Individual/Family Counseling	74	71	95.9
Substance Abuse Assessment	73	64	87.7
Health Services	74	64	86.5
Substance Abuse Counseling	73	62	83.8
Mentoring/Peer Support Group	74	59	79.7
Substance Abuse Treatment	74	57	77.0
Foster Care Prevention	74	30	70.5
Family Reunification	74	59	66.3
Support Services	**75**	**75**	**100.0**
Financial Counseling	75	88	90.7
Case Worker Follow-up: Housing	75	67	89.3
Child Care Assistance	75	63	84.0
Case Worker Follow-up: Mental/Physical Health	75	62	82.7
Case Worker Follow-up: Education	75	59	78.7
Case Worker Follow-up: Employment	75	59	78.7
Transportation Assistance	75	59	78.7
Legal Assistance	75	59	78.7
Clothing/Work Equipment Assistance	75	57	76.0

Table 4.17 (continued)

Program Areas and Components	n ($N = 78$)	Number of Programs	Percentage of Programs
Case Management	**75**	**74**	**98.7**
Needs Assessment	75	73	97.3
Coordination of Services	75	73	97.3
Service Plan	75	71	94.7
Permanent Housing Assistance	**75**	**74**	**98.7**
House/Search/Location Assistance	75	68	90.7
Housing Advocacy	75	62	82.7
Entitlement Assistance	75	61	81.3
Children's Programs	**74**	**71**	**95.9**
Counseling	74	66	88.0
Preschool and Child Care Programs	75	65	86.7
After-School Programs	75	62	82.7
Activities During Parent Meetings	75	66	74.6
Art/Play Therapy	75	45	60.0
Employment Training	**75**	**70**	**93.9**
Job Search Assistance	75	65	86.7
Job Readiness	75	61	81.3
Employability and Skills Assessment	75	61	81.3
Vocational and Occupational Skills Training	75	58	77.3

Table 4.17 (continued)

Program Areas and Components	n ($N = 78$)	Number of Programs	Percentage of Programs
Occupational Exploration	75	57	76.0
Individual Vocational Plan	74	56	74.7
Job Placement	75	53	70.7
Entrepreneurial Training	75	18	24.0
Cultural, Recreational, and Social Activities	**74**	**63**	**85.1**
Adult Basic Education	**74**	**63**	**85.1**
General Education Diploma	74	63	85.1
Computer Applications Education	74	59	79.7
Literacy Education	75	55	73.3
Math Skills Education	74	50	67.6
College Preparatory Guidance	75	52	64.0
Individual Education Plan	75	44	58.7
English-as-a-Second-Language	74	40	54.1

Note. Differences between valid n and N are caused by missing responses.

Employment Training was provided by 93.9% of the programs. Within this area, at least 81% of the programs provided all of the components with the exception of vocational and occupational skills training, occupational exploration, individual vocational plans, and job placement. Entrepreneurial training as a component was only provided by 24% of the programs.

Cultural and Recreational Activities were provided by 85.1% of the programs.

Adult Basic Education was provided by 85.1% of the programs in the form of classes leading to a general education diploma; nonetheless, 15% of the programs provided no adult basic education to their participants. At least 73% of the programs provided literacy and computer applications education. At least 64% of the programs provided college preparatory guidance and math skills education. At least 54% of the programs provided English-as-a-second language (ESL) classes and individual education plans.

The methods used in case management and support services follow-up are shown in Table 4.18. The most frequently used method of follow-up was phone calls with 88% of the respondents using this method. Home visits (74.7%), case management services (69.3%), mailings (62.7%), and support groups (49.3%) were other methods used frequently.

Table 4.18: Types of Case Management and Support Services Follow-up Available to Participants

Type of Service	Number of Programs	Percentage of Programs
Phone Call	66	88.0
Home Visit	56	74.7
Case Management Services	52	69.3
Mailings	47	62.7
Support Groups	37	49.3
Employer Visit	5	6.7

Note. Number of valid observations = 75. Missing responses = 3. Columns do not total 100% because of multiple responses.

As shown in Table 4.19, most components in Case Management and Support Services program areas were provided both during and after the program. About one-third of the programs provided case management services only during the program. The component provided most often during the program was transportation assistance by 62.5% of the programs.

The length of follow-up services in responding programs is shown in Table 4.20. One year of follow-up was provided in 47.2% of the programs. Twenty percent of the responding programs provided six months of follow-up. The U.S. Department of Housing and Urban Development's Supportive Housing Program funds up to six months of follow-up services after the participant moved into permanent housing. Program staff spent on average 18.81 hours per week on follow-up.

Table 4.19: When Case Management and Support Services Were Provided to Program Participants

Program Areas and Components	When Components Are Provided by %:		
	During Program	After Program	Both
Case Management	33.8	0.0	66.2
Needs Assessment	43.7	0.0	56.3
Service Plan	48.6	0.0	51.4
Coordination of Services	40.8	0.0	59.2
Support Services	23.0	1.4	75.6
Case Worker Follow-up: Housing	15.4	13.8	70.8
Case Worker Follow-up: Education	15.8	7.0	77.2
Case Worker Follow-up: Employment	23.2	8.9	67.9
Case Worker Follow-up: Mental/Physical Health	27.6	5.2	67.2
Transportation Assistance	62.5	1.8	35.7
Child Care Assistance	46.7	0.0	53.3
Clothing/Work Equipment Assistance	36.4	1.8	61.8
Legal Assistance	42.1	0.0	57.9
Financial Counseling	37.3	1.5	61.2

Table 4.20: Length of Follow-up Service

Length	Number of Programs	Valid Percentage
Less than Day	1	1.4
1 Month	1	1.4
3 Months	5	7.1
6 Months	14	20.0
1 Year	33	47.2
Over 1 Year	16	22.9
Total	70	100.0

Note. Number of valid observations = 70. Missing responses = 8.

The funding levels of follow-up services are indicated in Table 4.21. Responding programs reported that 41.4% of the programs did not have funding for their follow-up program. Fully funded follow-up services were provided by 37.2% of the programs and 21.4% of the programs were partially funded.

Table 4.21: Level at Which Follow-up Was Funded

Funding Level	Number of Programs	Valid Percentage
Fully Funded	26	37.2
Partially Funded	15	21.4
Not Funded	29	41.4
Total	70	100.0

Note. Number of valid observations = 70. Missing responses = 8.

The types of employment training provided in transitional programs are reported in Table 4.22. Of those that responded, 81% provide vocational/occupational skills training, 44.4% provide on-the-job training, and 39.7% provide work experiences and transitional employment.

The number of hours program participants spend weekly on employment training are shown in Table 4.23. Ten to 20 hours per week was spent by 44.4% of the responding programs. Twenty-one to 30 hours was spent in employment training by 27.8% of the responding programs and another 22.2% of the programs spent less than 10 hours per week in employment training.

Table 4.22: Types of Employment Training Provided in Programs

Types of Employment Training	Number of Programs	Percentage of Programs
Vocation /Occupational Skills Training	51	81.0
On-The Job-Training	28	44.4
Work Experience/Transitional Employment	25	39.7
Apprenticeship Program	17	27.0
Paid Internships	6	9.5
Mentoring Internships	5	7.9

Note. Number of valid observations = 63. Missing responses = 15. The columns do not total 100% because of multiple responses.

Table 4.23: Number of Hours Spent Per Week in Employment Training

Number of Hours	Number of Programs	Percentage of Total
Less than 10 hours	12	22.2
10-20 Hours	24	44.4
21-30 Hours	15	27.8
31-40 Hours	3	5.6
Total	54	100.0

Note. Number of valid observations = 54. Missing responses = 24.

Table 4.24: Job Placement Services Used in Programs

Job Placement Service	Number of Programs	Percentage of Programs
Self-Directed Job Search	43	71.7
Job Service/Employment Service	42	70.0
Newspaper	34	56.7
Vendor/Contractor/and Organizations	22	36.7
Job Banks	20	33.3

Note. Number of valid observations = 60. Missing responses = 18. Columns do not equal 100% because of multiple responses.

The type of job placement services used in responding programs are indicated in Table 4.24. Most programs used self-directed job searches (71.7%), job service or employment service (70.0%), and newspapers (56.7%).

Question 4: Where are program areas and components provided?

Where program areas and components were provided—on-site, off-site, or both—are shown in Table 4.25. More than 53% of the programs provided Adult Basic Education off-site with the exception of individual education plans, which were provided off-site by only 45.5% of the programs. More than 51% of the programs provided Employment Training off-site with the exception of individual vocational plans, which was provided off-site by 45.5% of the programs; occupational exploration, which was provided off-site by 42.1% of the programs; and job search assistance, which was provided off-site by 38.5% of the programs. More than 54% of the programs provided Family and Independent Living Skills Education on-site. Three components had less than the reported on-site percentage because they were provided both on-site and off-site. They were parenting education, child development and behavior management education, and domestic violence awareness. Legal issues education was provided off-site by 47.5% of the programs. Physical Housing Assistance was provided, generally, both on-site and off-site. More than 86% of the programs provided Family Health and Preservation services both on-site and off-site. Foster care prevention was provided off-site by 45.2% of the programs. Individual/family counseling, mentoring/peer support groups, and family reunification components were provided both on-site and off-site. Health services, substance abuse assessment, substance abuse treatment, and substance abuse counseling components were primarily provided off-site. Children's Programs provided most components both on-site and off-site with the exception of activities during parent meetings and art/play therapy, which were provided on-site. Cultural and Recreational Activities were usually provided both on-site and off-site.

The educational institutions where Adult Basic Education services were provided are reported in Table 4.26. Community college programs were used by 42.7% of the responding programs. The most common program listed under other programs was community-based adult basic

Table 4.25: Where Program Areas and Components Were Provided

Program Areas and Components	Where Provided by %		
	On-Site	Off-Site	Both
Adult Basic Education	**10.0**	**70.0**	**20.0**
Individual Education Plan	31.8	45.5	22.7
English-as-a-Second-Language	19.5	72.2	7.3
Literacy Education	18.2	67.3	14.5
Math Skills Education	22.0	62.0	16.0
General Education Diploma	16.1	61.3	22.6
Computer Applications Education	25.0	53.3	21.7
College Preparatory Guidance	14.2	59.2	26.5
Employment Training	**20.6**	**55.9**	**23.5**
Individual Vocational Plan	27.3	45.5	27.3
Occupational Exploration	22.8	42.1	35.1
Employability and Skills Assessment	23.3	51.7	25.0
Job Search Assistance	21.5	38.5	40.0
Job Readiness	18.0	52.5	29.5
Vocational and Occupational Skills Training	6.9	79.3	13.8
Entrepreneurial Training	23.5	64.7	11.8
Job Placement Location	11.8	52.9	35.3
Family and Independent Living Skills Education	**54.8**	**5.5**	**39.7**
Parenting Education	42.2	12.7	45.1
Child Development and Behavior Management Education	43.5	13.0	43.5
Child Abuse Awareness Education	57.4	14.8	27.8
Housing and Independent Living Education	72.7	1.5	25.8
Budget and Money Management Education	71.4	4.3	24.3

Table 4.25 (continued)

Program Areas and Components	Where Provided by %		
	On-Site	Off-Site	Both
Family and Independent Living Skills Education			
Credit and Debt Management Education	55.4	14.3	30.3
Time Management Education	74.1	5.6	20.3
Health and Hygiene Education	55.7	13.1	31.2
Nutrition Education	61.9	15.9	22.2
Stress Management Education	62.5	7.1	30.4
HIV/STD Awareness	54.7	20.3	25.0
Domestic Violence Awareness	42.9	15.9	41.2
Self Esteem, Motivation, and Attitude Development Education	50.0	6.9	43.1
Use of Community Resources Education	62.9	5.7	31.4
Legal Issues Education	31.1	47.5	21.4
Physical Housing Assistance	**31.1**	**8.1**	**60.8**
House/Search/Location Assistance	38.2	5.9	55.9
Entitlement Assistance	36.1	8.2	55.7
Housing Advocacy	41.9	8.1	50.0
Family Health and Preservation	**4.0**	**9.3**	**86.7**
Health Services	10.9	59.4	29.7
Individual/Family Counseling	22.5	29.6	47.9
Substance Abuse Assessment	16.9	63.1	20.0
Substance Abuse Treatment	3.5	82.5	14.0
Substance Abuse Counseling	9.7	59.7	30.6
Mentoring/Peer Support Group	33.9	28.8	37.3
Foster Care Prevention	19.4	45.2	35.4
Family Reunification	32.7	26.5	40.8

Table 4.25 (continued)

Program Areas and Components	Where Provided by %		
	On-Site	Off-Site	Both
Children's Programs	**44.1**	**15.3**	**40.6**
Preschool and Child Care			
Programs	32.8	39.1	28.1
After-School Programs	36.1	39.3	24.6
Counseling	30.3	31.8	37.9
Activities During Parent			
Meetings	78.6	3.6	17.8
Art/Play Therapy	63.6	25.0	11.4
Cultural, Recreational, and			
Social Activities	**11.1**	**20.6**	**68.3**

education. Programs at public high schools, vocational high schools, and shelter adult education programs, which were non Board of Education certificated, each were used by approximately 20% of the responding programs.

Table 4.26: Educational Institutions Where Adult Basic Education Was Provided

Educational Institution	Number of Programs	Percentage of Programs
Community Colleges	32	42.7
Other	19	25.3
Public High School	16	21.3
Vocational High School	16	21.3
Shelter Adult Education Program (Non BOE)	15	20.0
Shelter Alternative High School (BOE)	10	13.3

Note. Number of valid observations = 75. Missing responses = 3 Columns do not total 100% because of multiple responses.

Organizations that provided employment training for program participants are identified in Table 4.27. Vocational schools were used by 61% of the responding programs. Community college programs were used by 50.8% of the programs. The other primary providers of employment training programs were JTPA (47.5%) and State Welfare to Work Programs (47.5%).

Table 4.27: Organizations Which Provided Employment Training

Organization	Number of Programs	Percentage of Programs
Vocational School	36	61.0
Community College/Post Secondary Institution	30	50.8
Community College Vocational Training Center	30	50.8
JTPA Training Program	28	47.5
State Welfare to Work Program	28	47.5
Vocational Center	19	32.2
On Site Program	18	30.5
Sheltered Workshop	10	16.9

Note. Number of valid observations = 59. Missing responses = 19. The columns do not total 100 % because of multiple responses.

Question 5: Who provides the program area and component?

The program areas and component providers are shown in Table 4.28. Adult Basic Education and Employment Training area components were provided primarily by community agencies. Most Family and Independent Living Skills Education was provided by program staff or both program staff and community agencies. Those components provided primarily by program staff included housing and independent living education (60.3%), budget and money management education (59.7%), time management (66.1%), credit and debt management education (45.5%), and use of community resource education (55.7%). The components provided most by community agencies were domestic violence awareness (43.8%) and legal issues education (63.5%). Physical Housing Assistance was provided in most programs by both program staff and community agencies. The majority of components in Family Health and Preservation were offered both by community and agencies and programs staff. Health services (74.6%), substance abuse assessment (59.7%), substance abuse treatment (80%), and substance abuse counseling (60%) were provided by community based agencies. Children's programs were also offered by both community based agencies and program staff. Preschool and child care programs (45.3%) and after-school programs (42.6%) were provided by community

Table 4.28: Program Area and Component Providers

Program Areas and Components	Provided By:		
	Program Staff %	Community Agency %	Both %
Adult Basic Education	**6.7**	**75.0**	**18.3**
Individual Education Plan	34.1	40.9	25.0
English-as-a-Second-Language	12.5	75.0	12.5
Literacy Education	12.5	71.4	16.1
Math Skills Education	14.0	66.0	20.0
General Education Diploma	10.9	65.6	23.5
Computer Applications Education	23.4	53.3	23.3
College Preparatory Guidance	8.3	62.5	29.2
Employment Training	**17.6**	**58.9**	**23.5**
Individual Vocational Plan	25.0	46.4	28.6
Occupational Exploration	22.8	40.4	36.8
Employability and Skills Assessment	20.0	48.3	31.7
Job Search Assistance	23.4	42.2	34.4
Job Readiness	20.0	55.0	25.0
Employment Training			
Vocational and Occupational Skills Training	7.0	82.5	10.5
Entrepreneurial Training	11.7	76.5	11.8
Job Placement Location	12.0	54.0	34.0
Family and Independent Living Skills Education	**37.5**	**5.6**	**56.9**
Parenting Education Child Development and Behavior	20.8	23.6	55.6
Management Education	28.6	15.8	55.6
Child Abuse Awareness Education	37.7	18.0	44.3

Table 4.28 (continued)

Program Areas and Components	Provided By:		
	Program Staff %	Community Agency %	Both %
Housing and Independent Living Education	60.3	2.9	36.8
Budget and Money Management Education	59.7	8.4	31.9
Credit and Debt Management Education	45.5	16.4	38.1
Time Management Education	66.1	3.6	30.3
Health and Hygiene Education	43.5	11.3	45.2
Nutrition Education	35.9	23.4	40.7
Stress Management Education	48.2	8.9	42.9
HIV/STD Awareness	23.4	43.8	32.8
Domestic Violence Awareness	33.3	19.0	47.7
Self Esteem, Motivation, and Attitude Development Education	40.3	8.3	51.4
Family and Independent Living Skills Education			
Use of Community Resources Education	55.7	4.3	40.0
Legal Issues Education	14.3	63.5	22.2
Physical Housing Assistance	**31.9**	**6.9**	**61.2**
House/Search/Location Assistance	40.9	6.1	53.0
Entitlement Assistance	35.6	10.2	54.2
Housing Advocacy	45.0	8.3	46.7

Table 4.28 (continued)

Program Areas and Components	Provided By:		
	Program Staff %	Community Agency %	Both %
Family Health and Preservation	**1.4**	**11.0**	**87.6**
Health Services	1.6	74.6	23.8
Individual/Family Counseling	14.7	35.3	50.0
Substance Abuse Assessment	11.3	59.7	29.0
Substance Abuse Treatment	3.6	80.0	16.4
Substance Abuse Counseling	6.7	60.0	33.3
Mentoring/Peer Support Group	25.9	31.0	43.1
Foster Care Prevention	10.3	48.3	41.4
Family Reunification	27.1	25.0	47.9
Children's Programs	**35.6**	**15.3**	**49.1**
Preschool and Child Care Programs	26.6	45.3	28.1
After-School Programs	31.1	42.6	26.3
Counseling	27.7	33.8	38.5
Activities During Parent Meetings	61.1	14.8	24.1
Art/Play Therapy	52.4	33.3	14.3
Cultural and Recreational Activities	**14.3**	**12.7**	**73.0**
Case Management	**69.0**	**4.2**	**26.8**
Needs Assessment	75.0	2.9	22.1
Service Plan	83.6	3.0	13.4
Coordination of Services	65.2	2.9	31.9
Support Services	**54.9**	**4.2**	**40.8**
Case Worker Follow-up: Housing	78.7	1.6	19.7
Case Worker Follow-up: Education	72.2	3.7	24.1

Table 4.28 (continued)

Program Areas and Components	Provided By:		
	Program Staff %	Community Agency %	Both %
Support Services			
Case Worker Follow-up: Employment	62.5	8.9	28.6
Case Worker Follow-up: Mental/Physical Health	52.5	10.2	37.3
Transportation Assistance	56.4	16.4	27.2
Child Care Assistance	37.5	28.6	33.9
Clothing/Work Equipment Assistance	49.0	17.0	34.0
Legal Assistance	15.8	52.6	31.6
Financial Counseling	46.0	11.1	42.9

agencies. Components offered by program staff included activities during parent meetings (61.1%) and art/play therapy (52.4%). The Cultural, Recreational, and Social Activities program area was offered by both community based agencies and program staff. Case Management components were offered by program staff in at least 65.2% of the programs. Support Services components were offered primarily by program staff. Legal assistance was an exception with 52.6% of the programs using a community-based agency to provide this service.

Question 6: What is the perceived importance of each program area and component in transitional programs?

The programs directors' perceptions of the importance of each program area and component irregardless, of whether they had the program area and component or not, are shown in Table 4.29. The program directors were asked to rate each program area and component on the following scale: 1= Not Important; 2 = Somewhat Important; 3 = Important; 4 = Very Important; 5 = Extremely Important. Based on rated values of 3 and above, 100% of the respondents considered Case Management, Children's Programs, Family and Independent Living Skills Education, Support Services, and Family Health and Preservation important.

Table 4.29: Importance of Program Areas and Components

Program Areas and Components	% of Rated Values of 3 or higher	Mean Value	SD	_n_ (N = 78)
Case Management	**100.0**	**4.77**	**.45**	**74**
Needs Assessment	100.0	4.56	.55	72
Service Plan	98.6	4.52	.67	71
Coordination of Services	98.6	4.45	.73	73
Child Care Assistance	98.6	4.44	.77	72
Personal Housing Assistance	**98.7**	**4.71**	**.59**	**75**
House Search/Location Assistance	100.0	4.53	.67	73
Housing Advocacy	93.0	4.28	.94	71
Entitlement Assistance	95.8	4.27	.93	71
Children's Programs	**100.0**	**4.59**	**.60**	**71**
Preschool and Child Care Programs	97.2	4.57	.69	72
Counseling	100.0	4.46	.69	72
After-School Programs	100.0	4.39	.67	70
Activities During Parent Meetings	95.7	4.11	1.00	70
Art/Play Therapy	90.0	3.84	1.03	64

Table 4.29 (continued)

Program Areas and Components	% of Rated Values of 3 or higher	Mean Value	SD	n (N = 78)
Family and Independent Living Skills Education	**100.0**	**4.56**	**.56**	**73**
Parenting Education	100.0	4.71	.65	73
Housing and Independent Living Education	100.0	4.54	.68	69
Child Development and Behavior Management Education	98.5	4.51	.68	68
Self Esteem, Motivation, and Attitude Development Education	97.3	4.51	.73	74
Budget and Money Management Education	100.0	4.45	.65	73
Child Abuse Awareness Education	95.7	4.41	.81	70
Domestic Violence Awareness	95.8	4.26	.90	72
Use of Community Resources Education	100.0	4.26	.79	72
Credit and Debt Management Education	100.0	4.24	.72	67
Stress Management Education	94.3	4.17	.92	70
HIV/STD Awareness	91.5	4.11	1.04	71
Health and Hygiene Education	95.7	4.09	.85	79
Time Management Education	92.6	3.93	1.01	68
Nutrition Education	94.6	3.92	.90	74
Legal Issues Education	97.2	3.90	.94	71

Table 4.29 (continued)

Program Areas and Components	% of Rated Values of 3 or higher	Mean Value	SD	n (N = 78)
Employment Training	**94.5**	**4.45**	**.73**	**73**
Vocation and Occupational Skills Training	100.0	4.27	.76	70
Job Placement	95.5	4.26	.93	66
Job Search Assistance	100.0	4.25	.77	71
Employability & Skills Assessment	98.6	4.24	.83	72
Job Readiness	94.1	4.21	.91	68
Individual Vocational Plan	95.7	4.16	.88	70
Occupational Exploration	97.1	4.09	.86	70
Entrepreneurial Training	54.2	2.81	1.21	59
Support Services	**100.0**	**4.44**	**.69**	**73**
Case Worker Follow-up: Housing	98.6	4.28	.81	72
Financial Counseling	98.6	4.21	.79	71
Case Worker Follow-up: Mental Health	97.2	4.20	.89	71
Case Worker Follow-up: Education	97.1	4.17	.88	70
Case Worker Follow up: Employment	98.6	4.04	.86	70
Transportation Assistance	87.1	3.79	1.08	70
Legal Assistance	88.7	3.61	1.08	71
Clothing/Work Equipment Assistance	86.1	3.58	1.15	72

Table 4.29 (continued)

Program Areas and Components	% of Rated Values of 3 or higher	Mean Value	SD	n (N = 78)
Family Health and Preservation	**100.0**	**4.41**	**.61**	**75**
Substance Abuse Treatment	100.0	4.54	.65	68
Individual/Family Counseling	100.0	4.49	.62	73
Substance Abuse Counseling	98.6	4.49	.64	69
Substance Abuse Assessment	98.6	4.40	.73	72
Health Services	98.6	4.33	.80	72
Mentoring/Peer Support Group	97.2	4.13	.86	71
Family Reunification	85.7	3.74	1.07	70
Foster Care Prevention	96.9	3.34	1.14	64
Adult Basic Education	**98.6**	**4.37**	**.75**	**70**
General Education Diploma Preparation	98.6	4.31	1.02	71
Literacy Education		4.00	1.13	70
Individual Education Plan	81.4	3.87	1.10	67
English-as-a-Second-Language	72.5	3.70	1.34	69
Math Skills Education	89.6	3.58	1.06	67
Computer Applications Education	84.6	3.45	1.02	65
College Preparatory Guidance	75.4	3.29	1.16	65
Cultural, Recreational, and Social Activities	**94.4**	**3.80**	**.92**	**71**

Note. Scale for this question is: 1 = Not Important; 2 = Somewhat Important; 3 = Important; 4 = Very Important; 5 = Extremely Important. Differences between valid *n* and *N* are caused by missing responses.

Personal Housing Assistance was considered important by 98.7%; Adult Basic Education by 98.6%; Employment Training by 94.5%; and Cultural, Recreational, and Social Activities by 94.4% of the respondents.

The mean scores for the program areas were as follows: Case Management—4.77; Personal Housing Assistance—4.71; Children's Programs—4.59; Family and Independent Living Skills Education—4.56; Employment Training—4.45; Support Services—4.44; Family Health and Preservation—4.41; Adult Basic Education—4.37; and Cultural, Recreational and Social Activities—3.80.

Components considered important by 100% of the respondents included needs assessment, house search/location assistance, counseling, after school programs, parenting education, housing and independent living skills education, budget and money management education, use of community resources, credit and debt management education, vocational and occupational skills training, job search assistance, substance abuse treatment, individual/family counseling.

Most components were considered important by at least 90% of the respondents. Components considered important by less than 90% of the respondents included transportation assistance (87.1%), clothing/work equipment assistance (86.1%), entrepreneurial training (54.2%), family reunification (85.7%), individual education plan (81.4%), English-as-a-second-language (72.5%), math skills education (89.6%), computer applications education (84.6%), and college preparatory guidance (75.4%).

Question 7: What are the current programs' outcomes?

The outcome categories are based on those of the U.S. Department of Urban Development's Supportive Housing Program/Transitional Housing Program. The Supportive Housing Program/Transitional Housing Program's goal was to provide supportive services that would enable program participants to increase their residential stability, to increase their educational level, to improve their employment status, to increase their income, and have greater self-determination (Office of Policy Development and Research, 1995). Program directors in the study determined their program's success based on the percentage of participants who improved in the following outcome categories: increased residential stability, increased educational level, improved employment status, and increased income. The ranges for the percentage of participants who improved in each outcome category are as follows: 1 = less than 20%; 2 = 21-40%; 3 = 41-60%; 4 = 61-80%; and 5 = over 80%. The outcomes of present programs are reported in Table 4.30a and b.

The outcome with the highest mean was "increased residential stability" at 4.12, or 61-80% of participants. The other outcomes had means in the 21-40% outcome range. The percentages of programs in each participant improvement outcome range, for each outcome category, are presented in Table 4.30b. The "increased educational level" outcome category had programs distributed quite evenly in the outcome ranges from 21% through 80%, with 29.7 % of the programs in the 41-60% category. Most of the programs (79.4%) had an "increased residential stability" outcome category range from 61% through over 80%, with 43.8% the programs in the over 80% range. In the "improved employment status" outcome category, the majority of programs were in the 21% through 80% outcome ranges, with 35.6% of the programs in the 41-60% outcome range. In the "increased income" outcome category, the majority of the programs were in the 21 through 80% outcome ranges, with 34.3% of the programs in the 21-40% outcome range, 27.4 percent of the programs in the 41-60% outcome range, and 17.8% in the 61-80% outcome range.

Table 4.30: Current Program Outcomes

a. Mean Outcomes of Programs

Program Outcome	Mean Value	*n* (*N* = 78)
Increased Educational Level	2.76	74
Increased Residential Stability	4.12	73
Improved Employment Status	2.92	73
Increased Income	2.70	73

Note. Scale for number of participants in each outcome category: 1 = less than 20%; 2 = 21-40%; 3 = 41-60%; 4 = 61-80 %; and 5 = over 80%.
Differences between valid *n* and *N* are caused by missing responses.

b. Distribution of Programs Participant Improvement in Outcome Categories

Program Outcome	Participant Improvement by Program Distribution %				
	< 20%	21-40%	41-60%	61-80%	Over 80%
Increased Educational Level	18.9	21.6	29.7	24.4	5.4
Increased Residential Stability	1.4	8.2	11.0	35.6	43.8
Improved Employment Status	15.1	17.8	35.6	23.3	8.2
Increased Income	13.7	34.3	27.4	17.8	6.8

Note. Columns of figures are percentage of programs in each participant improvement outcome range.

Goal 3: Program Demographics, Program Areas, and Components Related to Successful Program Outcomes and Important in an Effective Transitional Program

In this section of the study, a direct comparison was made between the responses to questions exhibiting a relationship to each other using crosstabulations with chi-square as the statistical test. Chi-square is a nonparametric statistical test used to determine the statistical significance of the differences between the observed frequencies with the frequencies that would be expected from normative data. The null hypothesis was that the two variables were independent. If the observed significance level was less than .10 ($p < .10$), the null hypothesis that the two variables were independent was rejected at a 90% level of confidence. Crosstabulations or contingency tables were used to compare program demographics with both program outcomes and program areas and components.

Question 8: What are the demographics of programs with successful outcomes?

Comparisons between program descriptions and program outcomes are shown in Table 4.31a, b, and c. The following outcome categories were found to be significant: "increased educational level" ($p < .10$),

Table 4.31: Demographic Data That Have a Relationship to Successful Program Outcomes

a. Program Descriptions That Have a Relationship to Successful Program Outcomes: Program Description by Increased Educational Level

Program Description	n (N = 78) of Total	%	% of Participants Who Increased Their Educational Level				
		<20%	21-40%	41-60%	61-80%	Over 80%	
Transitional Shelter	20	27.0	30.0	15.0	30.0	25.0	
Emergency and Transitional Shelter	9		12.2	11.1	55.6	11.1	22.2
Transitional Housing	42	56.8	16.7	19.0	33.3	21.5	9.5
Other	3	4.0	33.5	66.5			
Total	74	100.0					

Note. Chi-square value = 2.83541. *p* = .09. Differences between valid *n* and *N* are caused by missing responses.

Table 4.31 (continued)

b. Program Descriptions That Have a Relationship to Successful Program Outcomes: Program Description by Improved Employment Status

Program Description	n (N = 78)	% of Total	% of Participants With Improved Employment Status				
			<20%	21-40%	41-60%	61-80%	Over 80%
Transitional Shelter	20	27.4	25.0	25.0	35.0	15.0.	
Emergency and Transitional Shelter	9	12.3	22.2	22.2	33.3	22.3	
Transitional Housing	41	56.2	9.8	14.6	34.1	26.8	14.7
Other	3	4.1	33.3	33.3	33.3		33.4
Total	73	100.0					

Note. Chi-square value = 7.84580. *p* = .005. Differences between valid *n* and *N* are caused by missing responses.

c. Program Descriptions That Have a Relationship to Successful Program Outcomes: Program Description by Increased Income

Program Description	n (N = 78)	% of Total	% of Participants Who Increased Their Income				
			< 20%	21-40%	41-60%	61-80%	Over 80%
Transitional Shelter	20	27.4	25.0	35.0	35.0	5.0	
Emergency and Transitional Shelter	9	12.3	22.2	33.3	22.2	11.1	11.2
Transitional Housing	41	56.2	7.3	34.1	24.4	26.8	7.4
Other	3	4.1		33.3	33.3		33.4
Total	73	100.0					

Note. Chi-square value = 6.56835. *p* = .01. Differences between valid *n* and *N* are caused by missing responses.

"improved employment status" ($p < .05$), and "increased income" ($p < .01$). Since all of these outcome categories had a significance level of .10 or less, the null hypothesis that the two variables were independent was rejected. In all three outcome categories, the program description "transitional housing" had more programs in the 61% through over 80% outcome range and the least percentage of programs in the less than 21% through 60% outcome range. No significant relationship was found between the outcome category "increased residential stability" and program description.

Comparisons between program size and the outcome category "improved education" are presented in Table 4.32. The outcome category "increased educational level" was significant ($p < .02$). Since this is less than .10, the null hypothesis that the two variables are independent was rejected. Programs in the outcome ranges above 61% were primarily programs with less than five individual family living units (50%) and 5-10 individual family living units (33.4%). Eighty percent of all programs with 21-25 individual family living units had outcomes in the less than 20% through 40% ranges. Even though 28.6% of the programs with over 25 individual family living units were in the over 61% outcome ranges, 64.3% of the programs with over 25 individual family living units had outcomes in the less than 20% through 40% outcome ranges. A significant relationship was not found between outcome categories "increased residential stability," "improved employment status," and "increased income" with the number of individual family living units in the program.

There was no significant relationship between the program outcomes and program length. Outcomes were not significantly different in any of the three geographical locations.

Comparisons between program descriptions and the program areas and components are presented in Table 4.33. Crosstabulations were done on each program areas and component. The program components in Table 4.33 had significant chi-square values; therefore, have a possible relationship to program descriptions. The null hypothesis was rejected due to a significance level of less than .10 ($p < .10$) in each of the seven listed components, with a 90% confidence level.

A majority of the responding programs had all of the components listed in Table 4.33. Case worker follow-up—housing; substance abuse counseling; art/play therapy; vocational and occupational skills training; cultural, recreational, and social activities; and child development and behavior management education were more likely not to be components in transitional housing programs than in transitional shelters, even emergency and transitional shelter programs. The only exception was computer application education, which was slightly more likely to be a component in transitional housing programs.

Comparisons between program length and the program areas and components are shown in Table 4.34. Crosstabulations were done on each program area and component. The significance level was less than .10 ($p <.10$) in one program area and four components. Therefore, the null hypothesis that the two variables were independent was rejected with a 90% confidence level.

A majority of responding programs had the program areas and components shown in Table 4.34. Only five responding programs did not have the program area employment training. Of the programs that had employment training, 50.8% were 13-24 months long, 26.1% were 1-6 months long, and 18.8% were 7-12 months long. Case worker follow-up—employment had a similar distribution as employment training; however, programs that did not have the case worker follow-up—employment were just as likely to have the same length of category distribution. Programs in which computer applications education was available reported that 40.6% were 13-24 months long, 30.5% were 1-6 months long, and 25.5% were 7-18 months long. Job search assistance was more likely to occur in programs over 19 months in length. Substance abuse counseling was more likely to occur in programs over 19 months long and less likely to occur in programs under six months long.

Comparisons between program individual family living unit numbers and the program areas and components are presented in Table 4.35. Crosstabulations were done on each program area and component. The significance level was less than .10 ($p < .10$) in each of the seven listed components. The null hypothesis that the two variables were independent was rejected with a 90% confidence level.

Case worker follow-up—education and substance abuse treatment was more likely to occur in programs with 5 to 10 individual family living units and less likely to occur in programs of less than 5 individual family living units. Legal assistance and credit and debt management was more likely to occur in programs with 5 to 10 individual family living units and less likely to occur in programs with less than five or over 25 individual family living units. Job readiness was more likely to occur in programs with 5 to 10 individual living

Table 4.32: Programs Size's Relationship to Successful Program Outcomes: Program Size by Improved Educational Level

Number of Units	n (N = 78)	Percent of Total	% of Participants Who Improved Their Education Level				
			<20%	21-40%	41-60%	61-80%	Over 80%
Less than 5	8	10.8	12.5	25.0	12.5	37.5	12.5
5-10	27	36.5	7.4	14.8	44.4	29 6	3.8
11-15	13	17.5	23.1	15.2	38.6	23.1	
16-20	7	9.5	14.3	28.6	28.6	14.3	14.2
21-25	5	6.8	40.0	40.0	20.0		
Over 25	15	18.9	35.7	28.6	7.1	21.4	7.2
Total	74	100.0					

Note. Chi-square value = 5.54129. *p* = .01. Differences between valid *n* and *N* are caused by missing responses.

Table 4.33: Components That Were Related to Program Description

| Program Component | Available | n | Percentages of Programs in Description Category | | | | DF | Chi-square Value | p |
			Transitional Shelter	*E & T Shelter	Transitional Housing	Other			
Case Worker Follow-up:	No	13		7.7	92.3				
Mental/Physical Health	Yes	62	32.3	12.9	50.0	4.8	3	11.97265	.00748
Substance Abuse	No	12		17.7	82.3				
Counseling	Yes	61	32.8	9.8	52.5	4.9	3	10.13990	.01741
Art/Play	No	29	10.3	24.1	62.2	3.4			
Therapy	Yes	43	34.9	4.7	55.8	4.6	3	10.13527	.01745
Vocational and	No	17	5.9	23.5	70.6				
Occupational Skills									
Training	Yes	57	33.3	8.8	52.6	5.3	3	9.20397	.02670
Computer	No	15	13.3	33.3	53.4				
Application Education	Yes	59	30.5	6.8	57.6	5.1	3	9.04033	.02876
Cultural, Recreational, and	No	11		18.2	81.8				
Social Activities	Yes	61	29.5	11.5	54.1	4.9	3	8.38020	.03877
Child Development &	No	11	18.2	9.1	63.6	9.1			
Behavior Management	Yes	63	28.6	11.1	57.1	3.2	1	2.74749	.09741
Education									

Note. *E & T (Emergency and Transitional) N = 78. Differences between valid n and N are caused by missing responses.

Table 4.34: Program Areas and Components That Were Related to Program Length

Program Areas and Components	Available	n	Percentage of Programs in Length Category					DF	Chi-square Value	p
			1-6 Months	7-12 Months	13-18 Months	19-24 Months	Over 24 Months			
Employment Training	No	5	40.0		60.0					
	Yes	69	26.1	18.8	11.6	39.2	4.3	4	10.79874	.02892
Case Worker Follow-up:	No	16	25.0	6.3	37.5	31.2				
Employment	Yes	59	27.1	20.3	8.5	39.0	5.1	4	9.70774	.04565
Computer Applications	No	15	13.3	40.0	20.0	20.0	6.7			
Education	Yes	59	30.5	11.9	13.6	40.6	3.4	4	8.74637	.06776
Job Search Assistance	No	10	40.0	10.0	40.0	10.0				
	Yes	64	25.0	18.8	10.9	40.6	4.7	4	8.70303	.06897
Substance Abuse Counseling	No	12	41.7		25.0	33.3				
	Yes	61	23.0	21.3	13.1	37.7	4.9		7.79895	.09923

Note. $N = 78$. Differences between valid n and N are caused by missing responses.

Table 4.35: Components That Related to Number of Individual Family Living Units in the Program

Program Component	Available	n	<5 Units	5-10 Units	11-15 Units	16-20 Units	21-25 Units	Over 25 Units	DF	Chi-square Value	p
Case Worker Follow-up:	No	16	37.5	25.0	18.8	6.2	6.2	6.3			
Education	Yes	59	3.3	40.7	16.9	10.3	6.8	22.0	5	16.47391	.00561
Legal Assistance	No	16	31.3	18.8	12.5	6.2	6.2	25.0			
	Yes	59	5.1	42.4	18.6	10.2	6.8	16.9	5	10.88355	.05374
Job Readiness	No	14	7.1	21.4	21.4	7.1	7.1	35.9			
	Yes	60	11.7	41.7	15.0	10.0	6.6	15.0	1	3.16309	.07532
Credit and Debt Management	No	14	28.6	21.4	7.1	7.1	7.1	28.7			
Education	Yes	59	5.1	40.7	20.3	10.2	6.8	16.9	5	9.65642	.08558
English-as-a-Second-Language	No	34	14.7	23.5	17.6	17.6	5.9	20.7			
	Yes	40	7.5	50.0	17.5	2.5	7.5	15.0	5	9.64925	.08581
Activities While Parents	No	19	15.8	36.8	15.8	5.3	10.5	15.8			
in Meetings	Yes	53	9.4	37.7	17.0	11.3	5.7	18.9	1	2.81542	.09336
Substance Abuse Treatment	No	17	29.3	29.4	11.8	5.9	11.8	11.8			
	Yes	56	5.4	39.2	17.9	10.7	5.4	21.4	5	9.25817	.09920

Note. $N = 78$. Differences between valid n and N are caused by missing responses.

units and less likely to occur in programs over 25 individual family living units. English-as-a-second-language (ESL) was more likely to occur in programs with 5 to 10 individual family living units. Activities while parents are in meetings were more likely to occur in programs of less than five individual family living units.

Question 9: Which program areas and components are present in programs with successful outcomes?

The results of the one-way analysis of variance, which tested the null hypothsis that the mean number of program components in each program area were equal in all program outcome ranges, are shown in Table 4.36. Tests conducted compared the mean number of components in the nine program areas with each of the four program outcomes. The null hypothesis was rejected at an alpha level of less than .10 ($p < .10$), with a 90% confidence level, for the following program areas and outcomes: Adult Basic Education had significant F values in the program outcomes "increased educational level" (2.430) ($p = .056$) and "improved employment status" (2.409) ($p = .058$). Employment training had a significant F value in the program outcomes "improved employment status" (2.670) ($p = .039$) and "increased income" (3.069) ($p = .041$). The program outcome "increased educational level," with Adult Basic Education as the program area, had the fewest mean number of components in the 21-40% program outcome range and the largest mean number of components in the over 80% program outcome range. The program outcome "improved employment status" in both Adult Basic Education and Employment Training had the smallest mean number of program components in the less than 20% outcome range and the largest mean number of components in the 61-80% outcome range. The program outcome "increased income" had the smallest mean number of components in the less than 20% outcome range and the largest mean number of program components in the over 80% outcome range.

A Scheffe´ test was done on the ANOVA results where the F ratio was statistically significant. The Scheffe´ is a special t-test, which takes into account that the researcher may find significant results because multiple comparisons were made on the same data, so it controls for the errors that may occur in the multiple comparisons. The t-test determines if there is a true difference in the means and determines which means are different from each other. The Scheffe´ test determined there were significant differences in the means at the .05 alpha level for all results with significant F ratios.

The comparisons between program areas and components and the program outcome "increased educational level" are shown in Table 4.37. Crosstabulations were done on each program area and component. The null hypothesis that the two variables were independent was rejected for one program area and 12 components. They had observed significance levels that were less than .10 (p < .10) with a 90% confidence level. Most programs had the program area and all of the components. Case worker follow-up—employment, math skills education, college preparatory guidance, computer application education, **Adult Basic Education**, child abuse awareness education, legal issues education, house search/location, English-as-a-second-language, housing advocacy, and preschool and child care programs had higher percentages of programs in the 41% through the over 80% outcome ranges. Those programs that did not have the program area Adult Basic Education and the other program components were more likely to have outcomes in the less than 20% through 60% outcome ranges. Most of the programs included the components—activities while parents were in meetings and foster care prevention. The programs had an equal possibility of successful outcomes whether they had these program components or not. If the program provided activities while parents were in meetings, a higher percentage of programs was more likely to be in the less than 20% outcome range. If the program provided foster care prevention, a higher percentage of programs was more likely to be in the over 80% outcome range.

The comparisons between program areas and components and the program outcome "increased residential stability" are presented in Table 4.38. Crosstabulations were done on each program area and component. The observed significance level was less than .10 (p < .10) in each of the seven components in Table 4.38, so the null hypothesis that the two variables are independent was rejected with a 90% confidence level. Most programs had the seven components that are listed in Table 4.38. Over 94% of the programs that did not have substance abuse treatment, substance abuse counseling, and health services components were found to have outcome ranges of 61% through over 80%. Over 75% of the programs with these components had outcome ranges of 61% through over 80%. This may suggest that programs without the components do not have participants with

Table 4.36: Analysis of Variance of Number of Program Components in Each Program Area by Program Outcomes

Program Outcome and Component Area	Mean of n	Mean Number of Components in Outcome Range					F	p
		<20	21-40	41-60	61-80	Over 80		
Increased Educational Level								
Adult Basic Education	5.14	5.14	3.75	5.77	5.39	6.00	2.430	.056
Improved Employment Status								
Adult Basic Education	5.11	4.09	5.85	4.58	6.12	4.83	2.409	.058
Employment Training	5.84	3.91	6.31	6.00	6.41	6.00	2.670	.039
Increased Income								
Employment Training	5.84	3.70	5.92	6.45	6.08	6.60	3.096	.041

Table 4.37: Program Area and Components That Improve Program Outcomes: Component by Improved Educational Level

Program Area and Components	Available	n	<20	21-40	41-60	61-80	Over 80	DF	Chi-square Value	p
						% of Participants Who Improved Education				
Case Worker Follow-up: Employment	No	16	12.5	43.8	43.7			4	16.33247	.00260
	Yes	58	20.7	15.5	25.9	31.0	6.9			
Math Skills Education	No	24	16.7	45.8	25.0	8.3	4.2	4	13.30711	.00987
	Yes	49	20.4	10.2	32.7	30.6	6.1			
Activities While Parents are in Meetings	No	19	10.5	26.3	31.6	26.3	5.3	8	18.16066	.02005
	Yes	52	21.2	21.2	28.8	23.0	5.8			
College Preparatory Guidance	No	26	26.9	30.9	19.2	19.2	3.8	1	3.96929	.04634
	Yes	48	14.6	16.7	35.4	27.0	6.3			
Computer Application Education	No	15	26.7	40.0	20.0	13.3		1	3.95756	.04666
	Yes	58	17.2	17.5	32.5	25.9	6.9			
Adult Basic Education	No	15	6.7	46.7	20.0	26.6		4	8.88080	.06415
	Yes	59	22.0	15.3	32.2	23.7	6.8			
Child Abuse Awareness Education	No	9	22.2	55.6	11.1	11.1		4	8.50794	.07465
	Yes	63	19.0	15.9	31.7	27.1	6.3			
Legal Issues Education	No	11	45.5	18.2	9.1	27.2		1	3.16172	.07538
	Yes	66	21.2	19.7	30.3	25.8	3.0			

Table 4.37 (continued)

Program Area and Components	Available	n	% of Participants Who Improved Education					DF	Chi-square Value	p
			<20	21-40	41-60	61-80	Over 80			
House Search/Location	No	7	42.9	28.6	14.3	14.2	6.0	1	3.11573	.07754
	Yes	66	16.7	21.2	30.3	25.8	5.8			
English-as-a-Second-Language	No	34	23.5	32.6	20.5	17.6	5.0	4	8.35656	.07936
	Yes	39	15.4	10.3	38.5	30.8				
Housing Advocacy Availability	No	13	38.5	23.1	15.4	23.0	6.6	1	3.06301	.08009
	Yes	60	15.0	21.7	31.7	25.0				
Preschool & Child Care Program	No	10	40.0	20.0	40.0	21.3	6.5	4	7.96892	.09273
	Yes	16	21.3	19.7	31.2	26.2				
Foster Care Prevention	No	42	21.5	19.0	33.3	20.0	13.3	4	7.91131	.09488
	Yes	30	16.7	23.3	26.7					

Note. $N = 78$. Differences between valid n and N are caused by missing responses.

substance abuse or health problems; therefore, the program components have a relationship to successful residential stability outcomes. Substance abuse treatment, substance abuse counseling, and health services also had a relationship to successful residential stability outcomes in programs with the component; therefore, these programs may have had participants with substance abuse and health problems. Activities while parents are in meetings, entitlement assistance, individual education plans, and housing and independent living education had higher percentages of programs in the 61% through over 80% outcome range.

The comparisons between program areas and components and the program outcome "improved employment status" are reported in Table 4.39. Crosstabulations were done on each program area and component. The observed significance level was less than .10 ($p < .10$) in the each of five components listed in Table 4.39, so the null hypothesis that the two variables were independent was rejected with a 90% confidence level. Most programs had the five components shown on Table 4.39. The percentage of programs in the 61% through over 80% outcome ranges was case worker follow-up—education (29.9%), after school programs (35.1%), employability and skills assessment (36.2%), domestic violence awareness (36.6%), child abuse awareness education (35.4%). Those programs that did not have these components had a lower percentage of programs in the higher outcome ranges.

The comparisons between program areas and components and the program outcome "increased income" are shown in Table 4.40. Crosstabulations were done on each program area and component. The observed significance level of each of the eight components listed in Table 4.40 was less than .10 ($p < .10$), so the null hypothesis that the two variables were independent was rejected. Most of the programs had the eight components shown in Table 4.40. The following were the percentages of programs that had the component in the 61% through over 80% outcome range: job placement (29.4%), job readiness (27.6%), employability and skills assessment (27.6%), case worker follow-up: education (26.3%), child abuse awareness education (25.8%), job search assistance (25.8%), credit and debt management education (23.2%), and mentoring and peer support groups (23.2%). The majority of the programs without these components had "increased income" outcomes in the less than 20-40% outcome range.

Table 4.38: Components That Improve Program Outcomes: Component by Increased Residential Stability

Program Component	Available	n	% of Participants Who Improved Residential Stability					DF	Chi-square Value	p
			<20	21-40	41-60	61-80	Over 80			
Substance Abuse Treatment	No	17			5.9	35.3	58.8	1	3.63117	.05617
	Yes	54	1.9	11.1	11.1	37.0	38.9			
Activities While Parents are in Meetings	No	19		5.3	21.1	26.3	47.3	8	14.19404	.07685
	Yes	51	2.0	9.8	7.8	39.2	41.2			
Substance Abuse Counseling	No	12				41.7	58.3	1	3.01635	.08243
	Yes	59	1.7	10.2	11.9	35.6	40.6			
Health Services	No	9				33.3	66.7	1	3.01037	.08273
	Yes	62	1.6	9.7	11.3	37.1	40.3			
Entitlement Assistance	No	12	8.3	8.3	16.7	41.7	25.0	1	2.98817	.08387
	Yes	60		8.3	10.0	33.4	48.3			
Individual Education Plan	No	30		3.3	20.0	26.7	50.0	4	8.13502	.08676
	Yes	43	2.3	11.6	4.7	41.9	39.5			
Housing & Independent Living Education	No	6		33.3	16.7		50.0	4	8.01232	.09113
	Yes	66	1.5	6.1	9.1	39.4	43.9			

Note. $N = 78$. Differences between valid n and N are caused by missing responses.

*Question 10: Which program demographics, program area, and
components are important in an effective transitional program model?*

Those findings that had significant relationships to successful program
outcomes are summarized in Table 4.41. The percentage of programs
that currently had the program area and component, and its mean
importance as perceived by the program directors, are also shown in
Table 4.41. The study results indicated that 24 components in seven
program areas had significant relationships to successful program
outcomes. The seven program areas included Personal Housing
Assistance, Children's Programs, Family and Independent Living Skills
Education, Employment Training, Support Services, Family Health and
Preservation, and Adult Basic Education. Programs with a size of 5-10
individual family living units and a length of 19-24 months had
statistically significant relationships to successful program outcomes
and had statistically significant relationships to the provision of 12 of
the 24 significant components.

Adult Basic Education and Employment Training were the two
program areas that had statistically significant differences in the mean
number of program components offered. In other words, programs with
more components in the Adult Basic Education and Employment
Training program areas appeared to have a higher number of
participants increase their educational level (ABE), improve their
employment status (ABE, Employment Training), and increase their
income (Employment Training). The Adult Basic Education program
area and five of the seven components in that area were found to have a
relationship to increased educational levels. Individual education plans
were related to increased residential stability. Four of the eight
components in Employment Training were found to have a relationship
to improved employment status or increased income. Employability
and skills assessment appeared to have a relationship to improved
employment status and increased income. Job search assistance, job
placement, and job readiness appeared to be related to increased
income.

A comparison of program areas and components that were perceived important by program directors are compared to the findings in
this study and shown in Table 4.42. The components were derived from
the directors' perception of important components (Table 4.29). There
are five program areas and 13 specific program components listed.

Those program areas and components were perceived as important by 100% of the program directors. Those are also the program areas and components with the highest importance means. Five of the nine program areas were specifically perceived important by the directors, and the 13 components came from seven of the nine programs areas. The program areas were Case Management, Children's Programs, Family and Independent Living Skills Education, Support Services, Family Health and Preservation Services (on list), and Employment Training (not on list). The two program areas not on the list are Adult Basic Education and Cultural, Recreational, and Social Activities.

The study found that seven of the nine program areas had statistically significant components. Adult Basic Education was the only program area that was specifically found to have a significant relationship to successful outcomes. Case Management and Cultural, Recreational, and Social Activities were the two areas without any components with relationships to successful outcomes.

Six of the 13 program components on the list were found to have significant relationships to outcomes. They were housing and independent living skills education, substance abuse treatment, house search/location assistance, after school programs, job search assistance, and credit and debt management education.

Table 4.39: Components That Improve Program Outcomes: Component by Improved Employment Status

Program Component	Available	n	% of Participants Who Improved Employment					DF	Chi-square Value	p
			<20	21-40	41-60	61-80	Over 80			
After-School Children's Program	No	13	15.4		69.2	7.7	7.7			
	Yes	57	15.8	21.1	28.0	26.3	8.8	4	11.20276	.02438
Case Worker Follow-up: Education	No	16		18.8	43.8	37.4				
	Yes	57	19.3	17.5	33.3	19.4	10.5	4	10.36705	.03468
Domestic Violence Awareness	No	12	8.3	25.0	58.3		8.3			
	Yes	60	16.7	16.7	30.0	28.3	8.3	4	9.07911	.05915
Employability & Skills Assessment	No	14	35.7	7.1	42.9	14.3				
	Yes	58	10.3	20.7	32.8	25.9	10.3	1	3.96208	.04657
Child Abuse Awareness Education	No	9	44.5	11.1	33.3		11.1			
	Yes	62	11.3	19.4	33.9	27.4	8.0	4	9.02261	.06954

Note. $N = 78$. Differences between valid n and N are caused by missing responses.

Table 4.40: Components That Improve Program Outcomes: Component by Increased Income

Program Component	Available	n	% of Participants Who Improved Income					DF	Chi-Square Value	p
			<20	21-40	41-60	61-80	Over 80			
Job Placement	No	21	28.6	47.6	14.3	4.8	4.7			
	Yes	51	7.8	29.4	33.4	21.6	7.8	1	8.04376	.00457
Job Readiness	No	14	35.7	42.9	14.3	7.1				
	Yes	58	8.6	32.8	31.0	20.7	6.9	1	6.37462	.01158
Employability and Skills Assessment	No	14	35.7	35.7	21.4	7.2				
	Yes	58	8.6	34.5	29.3	19.0	8.6	1	6.37462	.01158
Case Worker Follow-up:	No	16		31.3	50.0	18.7				
	Yes	57	17.5	35.1	21.1	17.5	8.8	4	10.79050	.02902
Child Abuse Awareness	No	9	33.4	44.4	11.1	11.1				
Education	Yes	62	11.3	33.9	29.0	17.7	8.1	1	3.68223	.05500
Job Search Assistance	No	10	30.0	50.0	10.0		10.0			
	Yes	62	11.3	32.3	30.6	19.4	6.4	1	3.09972	.07831
Credit and Debt Management	No	14	21.4	50.0	21.5		7.1			
Education	Yes	57	12.3	31.6	28.1	21.0	7.0	1	2.90670	.08821
Mentoring and Peer Support	No	15	26.7	26.7	13.3	33.3				
Groups	Yes	56	10.7	35.7	30.4	14.3	8.9	4	8.02240	.09076

Note. N = 78. Differences between valid n and N are caused by missing responses.

Table 4.41: Effective Program Areas, Components, and Demographics

Program and Components	% of Programs with Impt. Area/Compoent	Mean	Statistically Significant Program: Outcomes	Statistically Significant Program: Demographics
Permanent Housing Assistance	**98.7**			
House Search/Location Assistance	90.7	4.53	Education	
Housing Advocacy	82.7	4.28	Education	
Entitlement Assistance	81.3	4.27	Residential	
Children's Programs	**95.9**			
Preschool and Child Care Programs	88.0	4.57	Education	
After-School Programs	86.7	4.39	Employment	
Family and Independent Living Skills Education	**100.0**			
Housing and Independent Living Education	100.0	4.54	Residential Education	5-10 Units
Child Abuse Awareness	87.7	4.41	Employment Income	5-10 Units
Domestic Violence Awareness	83.8	4.26	Employment	5-10 Units
Credit and Debt Management Education	80.8	4.24	Income	5-10 Units
Legal Issues Education	85.1	3.90	Education	

Table 4.41 (continued)

Program and Components	% of Programs with Impt. Area/Compoent	Mean	Statistically Signifcant Program: Outcomes	Statistically Signifcant Program: Demographics
Employment Training	**93.9**			
Job Placement	70.7	4.26	Income	
Job Search Assistance	86.7	4.25	Income	19-24 Months
Employability & Skills Assessment	81.3	4.24	Employment Income	
Job Readiness	81.3	4.21	Income	5-10 Units
Support Services	**100.0**			
Case Worker Follow-up: Education	78.7	4.17	Employment Income	5-10 Units
Case Worker Follow up: Employment	78.7	4.04	Education	19-24 Months
Family Health and Preservation	**100.0**			
Substance Abuse Treatment	77.0	4.54	Residential	5-10 Units
Health Services	98.6	4.33	Residential	
Mentoring/Peer Support Group	79.7	4.13	Income	
Foster Care Prevention	70.5	3.34	Education	

Table 4.41 (continued)

Program and Components	% of Programs with Impt. Area/Compoent	Mean	Outcomes	Demographics
Adult Basic Education	85.1		Education	
Individual Education Plan	58.7	3.87	Residential	
English-as-a-Second-Language	54.1	3.70	Education	5-10 Units
Math Skills Education	67.6	3.58	Education	
Computer Applications Education	79.7	3.45	Education	19-24 Months
College Preparatory Guidance	64.0	3.29	Education	

Note. Importance means are program directors' perceptions. Scale for importance means was: 1 = Not Important; 2 = Somewhat Important; 3 =Important; 4 = Very Important; 5 = Extremely Important. Units refer to the number of individual family living areas in a program.

Table 4.42: Components Perceived Important by 100% of Program Directors

Importance Rank	Program Areas and Components	Importance Mean	Components Statistically Significant to Program Outcomes
1	**Case Management**	**4.77**	
2	Parenting	4.71	
3	**Children's Programs**	**4.59**	
4	Needs Assessment	4.56	
4	**Family and Independent Living Skills Education***	**4.56**	
6	Housing and Independent Living Skills Education	4.54	Education
6	Substance Abuse Treatment	4.54	Residential Stability
8	House Search/Location Assistance	4.53	Education
9	Individual and Family Counseling	4.49	
10	Counseling for Children	4.46	
11	Budget and Money Management Education	4.45	
12	**Support Services***	**4.44**	
13	**Family Heath and Preservation Services***	**4.41**	
14	After-School Programs	4.39	Employment
15	Vocational and Occupational Skills Training	4.27	
16	Use of Community Resources Education	4.26	
17	Job Search Assistance	4.25	Income
18	Credit and Debt Management Education	4.24	Income

Note. Program areas are in bold. * Denotes programs areas in which statistically significant program components were located.

CHAPTER 5

Summary, Conclusions, and Recommendations

SUMMARY

Family homelessness is one of the most profound and disturbing social problems of the 1990s and will be one of the most important issues facing the United States in the twenty-first century. Most homeless families are headed by single women who are victims of poverty; are disadvantaged by ethnic, educational, and income status; lack advanced education or job training; and are hampered by poor family functions in their family of origin. Thus, it follows that strengthening the mother is of primary importance so she can become self-sufficient and economically independent, and also positively impact her own child's development.

The main purpose of the study was to develop a transitional program framework that can assist homeless women with children to become self-sufficient. In order to create this framework, this study identified nine program areas containing a total of 58 components and four program outcome categories. The three goals of this study were:

Goal 1: To identify, characterize, and analyze the current transitional programs for homeless women with children.

Goal 2: To determine the current program areas and components, perceived program area and component importance, and program outcomes.

Goal 3: To determine which program demographics, program areas, and components are related to successful program outcomes and important in effective transitional programs.

A descriptive research methodology was used for data collection. A survey questionnaire was sent to program directors of transitional shelter/housing programs for homeless women with children in the 29 continental United States cities that participated in the 1994 U.S. Conference of Mayors' annual 30-city survey. The descriptive survey research involved systematic data collection in order to address questions concerning characteristics of the programs and participants; current program areas and components, including education and employment training components; importance of the program areas and components; and program outcomes.

In conducting the study, the researcher was confronted with several limitations. The director's perception of program importance could not be reliably compared to outcomes because directors who do not have the program component cannot accurately judge its importance to program outcomes. The research can, however, discuss how directors' perceptions of what are the most important program components compare with the findings of the study.

Present participants could not be compared with past outcomes because the outcomes reflect previous participant outcomes and the researcher had no demographic data on those participants. The new participants may have different profiles from previous participants. Nonetheless, the researcher is comfortable with making some generalizations because the study program participants match the profile of homeless women with children discussed in the literature.

CONCLUSIONS

Description of Current Programs

The majority of the programs described themselves as transitional housing programs with 5 to 15 individual family living units. One-third of these programs had a program length for participants of 19-24 months. The majority of the programs reported links with housing, welfare, or social service agencies; employment, mental health, and community non-profit service providers; and educational institutions and employment training programs. The U.S. Department of Housing and Urban Development's Supportive Housing Program/Transitional

Housing Program was ranked as the most important funding source by 48.5% of the programs. Other important sources of funding included private individuals and organizations, religious groups, and state and local governments.

Profile of Current Transitional Program Participants

The majority of the participants were women with children between the ages of 20 and 34. The majority of the women (85.8%) were minority women with children. Most of the women were single. The most frequent reasons for homelessness were physical abuse, housing issues such as eviction or the lack of affordable housing, lack of family support, and substance abuse. The average number of children in the homeless family was between two and three. Children five years or younger made up 58.8% of the children in the programs. The majority of the participants failed to graduate from high school or vocational technical school. The majority of the participants were either unemployed or had never been employed when they entered a program; however, program directors judged that 76.7% of the participants were probably or definitely employable. The reasons for the participants' unemployment, as perceived by their program directors, included lack of competitive employment skills, lack of education, lack of child care, lack of interpersonal skills, lack of communication skills, lack of employment opportunities, and lack of transportation.

Current Program Components

The homeless women with children were participants in transitional programs that provided 58 components in nine program areas. The majority of the programs provided all program areas and components. Follow-up services were provided by 47.2% of the programs for up to one year. Program staff spent approximately 19 hours per week providing follow-up services. Responding programs reported that 42.2% of the programs did not have funding for their follow-up program. Vocational and occupational skills training was provided by 81% of the responding programs. Ten to 20 hours per week was spent by 44.4% of the responding programs' participants in employment training. Most programs used self-directed job searches, job service/employment services, and newspapers as job placement services.

Programs provided program areas and components both on-site and off-site. More than 53% of the programs provided adult basic education off-site. Community college programs were used by 42.7% of the responding programs. More than 51% of the programs provided employment training off-site. Vocational schools and community colleges were used by over 50% of the programs to provide employment training. State Welfare to Work programs and JTPA programs were the other primary providers of employment training. More than 54.7% of the programs provided family and independent living skills education on-site. More than 59% of the programs provided family health and preservation services off-site. All other program area components were provided both on-site and off-site. Most components supplied on-site were provided by programs staff and most components provided off-site were made available by community agencies.

Directors' Perceptions of Component Importance

All of the program directors (100%) perceived the following five program areas and 13 components as important: Case Management, Support Services, Family Heath and Preservation Services, Family and Independent Living Skills Education, Children's Programs, parenting education, needs assessment, housing and independent living skills education, substance abuse treatment, house search/location assistance, individual and family counseling, counseling for children, budget and money management, after-school programs, vocational and occupational skills training, use of community resources education, job search assistance, and credit and debt management education.

Current Program Outcomes

The mean program outcomes levels (percentage of participant improvement) for "increased educational level," "improved employment status," and "increased income" were in the 21-40% outcome range. The mean for "increased residential stability" was in the 61-80% outcome range.

Effective Transitional Program Demographics and Components

The program description "transitional housing" had more programs in the 61-over 80% outcome ranges for the following outcome categories:

"increased educational level," "improved employment status," and "increased income." "Transitional housing" also had the least percentage of programs in the 20-60% outcome ranges. No significant relationship was found between the outcome category "increased residential stability" and program description. The "increased educational level" program outcomes were higher in programs of less than 10 units. Components related to programs with 5-10 units were case worker follow-up: education, substance abuse treatment, legal assistance, credit and debt management, job readiness, English-as-a-second-language (ESL), and activities while parents are in meetings. Employment Training program area components, as well as the substance abuse counseling component, were more likely to occur in programs that were 19-24 months long.

There were 24 components in seven program areas with significant relationships to effective program outcomes. Programs with a size of 5-10 units and a length of 19-24 months had significant relationships to successful programs and to 12 of the 24 significant components.

FRAMEWORK RECOMMENDATIONS

In order to create the framework, this study identified nine program areas containing a total of 58 components and four program outcome categories Program areas and components were compiled from the following sources: studies by Burt and Cohen (1989), DaCosta Nunez (1994), Institute for Children and Poverty (1994), Lam (1987), and Rossi (1989a, 1994b); United States government reports from the Department of Education (1993a); Department of Housing and Urban Development (1995), Department of Labor (1991, 1994), New York State Education Department (1990); and a review of the author's proposed components by the expert panel. The outcome categories were based on those of the U.S. Department of Urban Development's Supportive Housing Demonstration Program.

After statistical analysis of the data, the following recommendations and interpretations can be made as a framework for transitional programs that serve homeless women with children. This is not to say that these particular program demographics and components are the only reasons for successful programs, but that most successful programs will have these components. As shown in Table 5.1, the

Table 5.1: Program Framework

Program Area and Components	Statistically Significant Program: Outcomes	Demographics
Permanent Housing Assistance		
House Search/Location Assistance	Education	
Housing Advocacy	Education	
Entitlement Assistance	Residential	
Children's Programs		
Preschool and Child Care Programs	Education	
After-School Programs	Employment	
Family and Independent Living Skills Education		
Housing and Independent Living Education	Residential	5-10 Units
Child Abuse Awareness Employment Income	Education	5-10 Units
Domestic Violence Awareness	Employment	5-10 Units
Credit and Debt Management Education	Income	5-10 Units
Legal Issues Education	Education	
Employment Training		
Job Placement	Income	
Job Search Assistance	Income	19-24 Months
Employability & Skills Assessment Income	Employment	
Job Readiness	Income	5-10 Units
Support Services		
Case Worker Follow-up: Education Income	Employment	5-10 Units
Case Worker Follow up: Employment	Education	19-24 Months

Table 5.1 (continued)

Program Area and Components	Statistically Significant Program:	
	Outcomes	Demographics
Family Health and Preservation		
Substance Abuse Treatment	Residential	5-10 Units
Mentoring/Peer Support Group	Income	
Foster Care Prevention	Education	
Adult Basic Education	Education	
Individual Education Plan	Residential	
English-as-a-Second-Language	Education	5-10 Units
Math Skills Education	Education	
Computer Applications Education	Education	19-24 Months
College Preparatory Guidance	Education	

Note. Bold print denotes program areas.

framework is made up of 24 program components in seven program areas. The number of units in the program and the length of the program appear to have a relationship to successful outcomes.

Program length was not related to success in any particular outcome category, but was a factor in being able to provide three of the 24 components in the framework. Program size was related to increasing participants' educational level and related to successful outcomes in eight of the 24 components. These facts lead the researcher to recommend that transitional programs be smaller in size (5-10 individual family living units) and be 24 months in length.

The program areas with components that have a relationship to successful outcomes include Permanent Housing Assistance, Children's Programs, Family and Independent Living Skills Education, Employment Training, Support Services, Family Health and Preservation, and Adult Basic Education. The researcher recommends that the 24 components in the framework be part of any transitional program for homeless women with children. A surprising finding was that case management did not have a significant relationship to any program outcome category even though 98.7% of the programs had case management components and it was considered the most important program area. This is not to say that case management is not an integral part of locating, coordinating, and monitoring defined services to meet each participant's specific needs. Of particular importance in the framework is the relationship of adult basic education and employment training components to successful program outcomes. Many of the programs and program directors did not perceive Adult Basic Education and Employment Training as important to successful outcomes as the study results imply. Education and employment training components in transitional programs for homeless women with children have an important role in assisting the participants to achieve the goal of self-sufficiency. The significant components in those program areas support the premise that disadvantaged and disorganized families need intensive family-oriented services. Effective programs must have integrated skills training and education, combined with a strong network of support services.

These study findings lead to the following recommendations:

1. Transitional programs should be 5-10 individual family living units in size.

2. Transitional programs should be 24 months in length with an additional follow-up period.

3. Program areas that are important in transitional programs include Permanent Housing Assistance, Children's Programs, Family and Independent Living Skills Education, Employment Training, Support Services, Family Health and Preservation, and Adult Basic Education. Case Management should be used to locate, coordinate, and monitor defined services to meet specific participant needs.

4. Adult Basic Education and Employment training are program areas that assist the transitional program participants to become self-sufficient and should be part of transitional programs.

5. Components that should be part of transitional programs include the following: housing search/location assistance, housing advocacy, entitlement assistance, preschool and child-care programs, after-school programs, housing and independent living education, child abuse awareness, domestic violence awareness, credit and debt management education, legal issues education, job placement, job search assistance, employability and skills assessment, job readiness, caseworker follow-up education and employment, substance abuse treatment, mentoring and peer group support, foster care prevention, individual education plans, English-as-a-second-language

(ESL), math skills education, computer applications education, and college preparatory guidance.

FUTURE RESEARCH

More research is needed to understand the complex issues of family homelessness, to develop successful strategies to prevent homelessness, and to develop programs that assist homeless families to become self-sufficient. The ideas that follow are problems that need to be addressed.

A needed companion piece of research to this study is an in-depth qualitative study of program participants one year and five years after completion of the program. The study would identify the participants' opinions of program components and characteristics that helped them to succeed. The data from the participant's perspective would be compared to the program director's perceptions and results of this study.

The importance and value of follow-up services that provide a supportive network after a transitional program needs further research. An analysis of the types of follow-up programs and the benefit of investing in such a program should be explored.

Information on education and employment training for homeless women with children on all levels of the continuum of care is needed. The appropriate types of education and employment training, education and training methods, education and training locations, and job placement activities that best meet the needs of specific participant social, economic, demographic, and educational profiles need to be identified. Also, an assessment would need to be made to determine if current education and employment training programs are available to meet the needs of homeless women with children.

Educational strategies that target populations at risk of not completing their high school education should be studied. The majority of the homeless women in the study did not complete their high school education. The issues that are at the "core" of these young women not completing their high school education need further exploration. The social and educational reforms that would give these at-risk populations a better chance of success must be addressed in future research.

Vocational educators and the business community need to explore how best to meet the occupational education and training needs of women from economically disadvantaged populations. Research must be conducted on developing vocational education programs that address the specific needs with regard to supportive services—such as child care, psycho-social issues—such as development of self-esteem, and economic issues such as—employment that provides an adequate income to support themselves and perhaps a family.

A study should explore how the business community (especially those who employ economically disadvantaged populations such as the hospitality industry) addresses the education and employment issues facing economically and educationally disadvantaged women in the workforce.

Family is such an important factor in a person's life. Homeless women with children lack supportive family relationships. Further study could explore the background of the participants in respect to family of origin, welfare dependency, family structure breakdown, and abuse.

Most transitional programs use the services of community-based agencies and organizations. A study of successful community collaboratives could obtain important information for communities developing programs to address the issues of family homelessness.

A study is needed to explore the impact of government cutbacks in social welfare programs that provide transitional housing, education, and employment training programs to homeless women with children. The study would also examine the capability of alternative funding sources to continue these programs.

And finally, a study is needed to examine the cost effectiveness of the current program models based on participant outcomes and the rates of recidivism among the participants.

Definitions of Government Programs and Legislation

STUART B. MCKINNEY HOMELESS ASSISTANCE ACT

The Stuart B. McKinney Homeless Act (P.L. 100-77) became law in July 1987. It has been re-authorized as follows: November 1988, the Omnibus McKinney Homeless Assistance Act of 1988 (P.L. 100-628) and November 1990, McKinney Act (P.L. 101-645). These acts created a number of new programs to provide urgently needed assistance to protect and improve the lives and safety of the homeless. The Stuart B. McKinney Homeless Assistance Act (P.L. 100-77) also established the Federal Interagency Council on the Homeless, an independent agency within the Executive Branch. The U. S. Secretary of the Department of Housing and Urban Development (HUD) chairs the council and the U. S. Secretary of the Department of Health and Human Services (HHS) is the vice chair.

The McKinney Act includes programs that address the needs of homeless people by providing for emergency shelter and food, primary and mental health care, transitional and longer term housing, educational programs, job training, and alcohol and drug abuse programs. The McKinney Act adds to existing federal social welfare programs that support homeless persons such as SSI, SSDI, Aid to Dependant Children (AFDC), Food Stamps, and Medicaid. Over the years, many McKinney programs have been changed, some programs consolidated, and new programs have been added. Many of the McKinney programs are now on different reauthorization cycles.

FAMILY SUPPORT ACT (FSA)

The Family Support Act (FSA) was enacted in 1988. It is designed to strengthen the nations's child support enforcement system, to help welfare recipients move into the labor market, and to provide them with support service to facilitate that transition. FSA created a federal program called Job Opportunities and Basic Skills Training (JOBS) that is designed to help recipients of AFDC become self-sufficient.

U.S. DEPARTMENT OF LABOR (DOL)

Employment Service The public Employment Service, or Job Service, is a nationwide labor exchange system of over 2,100 local offices through which qualified applicants are referred to job openings submitted by employers. The program is authorized under the Wagner-Peyser Act, enacted in 1933, and is administered in most states under grants from the U. S. Department of Labor (DOL).

Unemployment Compensation (UC) The Social Security Act of 1935 created the federal-state unemployment compensation system to provide financial relief to workers who had lost their jobs recently and involuntarily, and to stabilize the economy during recession. States establish their own eligibility requirements, with criteria related to types of employers, length of employment, circumstances of leaving employment, availability for work, among other variables. The system is financed by taxing employers on a certain proportion of their payroll expenses. The regular benefits under the UC system cover two quarters (26 weeks). After regular benefits are exhausted, some programs provide extended benefits for an additional one or two quarters. The availability of extended supplemental benefits has often been tied to periods of economic downturn.

U.S. DEPARTMENT OF HOUSING AND URBAN DEVELOPMENT (HUD)

Community Development Block Grants (CDBG) These grants, authorized under Title I of the Housing and Community Development Act of 1974, are intended to develop viable urban communities by providing decent housing and a suitable living environment, and by expanding economic opportunities, principally for persons of low and moderate income, The funds are allocated by formula, to "entitlement communities," including central cities in metropolitan statistical areas and other cities with more than 50,000 population; and qualified urban counties with more than 200,000 population; and to states for use by non-entitlement communities. The funds may be used for a range of community development activities directed toward neighborhood revitalization, economic redevelopment, and improved community facilities and services.

Section 8 Rental Certificate Programs This program, originally authorized under the Housing and Community Development Act of 1974, is designed to provide decent, safe, and sanitary housing for low income families in private market rental units at affordable rents. It provides for housing assistance payments in the form of certificates issued by authorized public housing agencies to participating owners on behalf of their eligible tenants. These payments make up the difference between the approved rent due to the owner for the dwelling unit and the family's required contribution toward the rent.

Section 8 Voucher Program Using a similar program, also administrated by public housing agencies, the Section 8 Voucher Program provides for a standard local payment. Recipients are free to choose any rental housing and, depending on the amount of rent charged, to use the voucher to cover part of the cost.

Operation Bootstrap This is an administrative initiative undertaken by HUD designed to address the multiple needs of families facing various housing deficiencies in order to enable them to eventually become economically self-sufficient. Under the program, designated housing agencies are authorized to give preference in the awarding of Section 8 certificates and vouchers to individuals who participate in a coordinated program of education, training, and supportive services. Since 1989, more than 360 agencies have been approved to participate in this program.

U.S. DEPARTMENT OF HEALTH AND HUMAN SERVICES (HHS)

Aid to Families with Dependent Children (AFDC) Aid to Families with Dependent Children is an entitlement program that serves primarily single-parent families with children. AFDC was created by the Social Security Act of 1935 to provide cash welfare payments for needy children who have been deprived of parental support or care because their father or mother is absent from home continuously, is incapacitated, is deceased, or is unemployed. In 9 out of 10 AFDC families, no male is present and the mother is the only adult in the household (Burt, 1992). AFDC is a combined state-federal program. Each state defines its needs standard, sets benefit levels, establishes income and resource limits within federal guidelines, and administers the program. Benefit levels differ widely. Any family that meets state eligibility criteria is entitled to benefits; the program has no spending cap.

Community Services Block Grants (CSBG) These grants, originally authorized under the Omnibus Budget Reconciliation Act of 1981 (OBRA), are intended to provide services and activities having a measurable impact on the causes of poverty in communities where poverty is a particularly acute problem. The funds are allocated as block grants, by formula, to states. The states disburse the funds to "eligible entities"—primarily, locally based community action agencies and/or organizations that serve seasonal or migrant farm workers—that provide services to low-income individuals and families. The block grant approach gives each state flexibility in tailoring programs to the particular service needs in individual communities.

Medicare Medicare is a federally-administered health insurance program for the elderly. Eligibility is automatic for anyone eligible to receive Social Security benefits.

Medicaid Medicaid is a joint federal-state program of medical coverage for the indigent. Medicaid eligibility varies from state to state: in all states, persons on Aid to Families with Dependent Children (AFDC) are automatically Medicaid-eligible, but other eligibility criteria differ across states.

SOCIAL SECURITY ADMINISTRATION

Social Security Social Security includes all income transfer programs administered through the United States Social Security Administration, Old Age Survivors Insurance (OASI) is the primary benefit. Social Security lifted more than twice as many out of poverty between 1979 and 1988 as did the means-tested cash food and housing benefits (Burt, 1992).

SSI/SSDI SSI (Supplemental Security Income) and SSDI (Social Security Disability Insurance) are both federally administered income transfer programs with eligibility that varies from state to state. SSDI is available to disabled persons with an employment history, while SSI is available to the disabled without an employment history. SSI began in late 1974. It is an entitlement program that supplements the incomes of poor, aged, blind, or disabled people. At maximum, SSI brings an individual or a couple up to 75-89% of the poverty threshold. SSI is indexed to the Consumer Price Index in the same way as Social Security payments. Complicated program rules determine the precise level of benefit for a given recipient. Many states supplement federal SSI payments, which are uniform across the country.

DEPARTMENT OF AGRICULTURE (USDA)

Food Stamp Program (FSP) The Food Stamp Program is designed to enable poor households to purchase food that provides a nutritionally adequate low-cost diet. It is an entitlement program. It is the only federal program available to all poor people without restrictions based on household type. In 1995, one in seven Americans participated in the Food Stamp Program with 50% of the participants being children (Center on Budget and Policy Priorities, 1995). To qualify for food stamps, poor households must have gross incomes of no more than 130% of the poverty threshold, and net income, after allowable deductions of no more than 100% of the poverty threshold. For a family of three in 1995, the income level was $16,000.00 per year (Center on Budget and Policy Priorities, 1995). Coupons are issued that can be exchanged for food at grocery stores. Food stamps have been indexed for inflation since 1973, and available in all states since 1975.

As a result of legislative changes in 1981 and 1982, about one million persons lost FSP eligibility, and the remaining recipients suffered some loss of benefits. The Food Security of 1985, the Stewart B. McKinney Homeless Assistance Act of 1987, and the Hunger Prevention Act of 1988 liberalized benefit and eligibility rules, but the net effect on program participation has been relatively small. The Hunger Prevention Act of 1988 also took the historic step of authorizing across-the-board increases in the maximum benefit above any inflation adjustments. These increases benefit every food stamp household.

Food Stamp benefit levels are determined as follows. Every year the Department of Agriculture establishes the cost of a Thrifty Food Plan for households of different sizes. Food stamp recipient households are assumed to be able to spend 30% of their "counted" income on food. Each household then receives food stamp coupons worth the difference between this 30% of "counted" income and the cost of the Thrifty Food Plan for a household of its size. The Hunger Prevention Act of 1988 provisions added two percent to the inflation-adjusted value of the Thrifty Food Plan in 1989 and 1990, and three percent each year since 1991. The add-on provides an across-the-board increase in food stamp benefits to every recipient household, adjusted only for the size of household. Because the Thrifty Food Plan is defined to be low in relation to real food costs, food affordability has been a problem for food stamp households. Households spending more than half of their adjusted income (about 35 to 40% of gross income) on shelter costs may claim an additional deduction if the amount they pay for shelter exceeds half of the adjusted income threshold, up to a ceiling indexed for inflation. FSP is increasingly less able to meet recipients' nutritional needs, even though benefits are indexed to inflation in food prices and a deduction is permitted for excess shelter costs (Burt, 1992).

STATE AND COUNTY ASSISTANCE PROGRAMS

General Assistance (GA) General Assistance (GA) is also known as Public Relief, Home Relief, Poor Relief, and by other names. General Assistance is a number of local and state income transfer related benefit programs. It is the support of last resort for many needy people. It is not governed by an federal statutes, and states are under no obligation or incentive to offer general assistance. Some states provide no mandate or standard; others allow counties to decide whether or not to offer a program that meets state standards; still others require all counties to provide programs that meets state standards; and some states administer their own programs. States and counties also vary in their rules for GA eligibility. Some allow able-bodied individuals to receive benefits (they usually require work or search for work); others restrict GA to the disabled and /or elderly not otherwise eligible for SSI; still others use GA only as a stopgap measure to help people cope until their AFDC or SSI applications are approved. GA benefits rarely provide the level of support available through AFDC or SSI.

MANPOWER TRAINING PROGRAMS

Manpower Development and Training Act of 1962 (MDTA) The Manpower Development and Training Act of 1962 aimed to improve the employability of the structurally unemployed (persons who lack the skills, education and other qualifications to complete successfully in the job market.

Economic Opportunity Act of 1964 (EQA) The Economic Opportunity Act of 1964 was a counter-cyclical program for persons whose joblessness was due to downturns in the business cycle.

Emergency Employment Act of 1971 (EEA) The Emergency Employment Act of 1971 aimed to improve the employability of the structurally unemployed. Those persons who lacked the skills, education, or other qualifications to complete successfully in the job market.

Comprehensive Employment Training Act of 1973 (CETA) CETA was a creative consolidation on the federal government's manpower training programs. It was shaped by the confluence of two major forces—one pragmatic, and the other ideological. First the United States Congress and the federal manpower administrators were dissatisfied with the patchwork of uncoordinated programs and reforms. Secondly, the Nixon administration had embraced the philosophy of the New Federalism and sought to decentralize a number of federal programs through block grant funding. CETA shifted authority from the federal government to state and local entities and consolidated these separate programs into block grants designed to provide responsibility in meeting local needs.

CETA's basic concepts were decentralization and de-categorization. Decentralization meant the transfer of authority for manpower programs from the federal government to the state and local government. De-categorization provided prime sponsors with flexibility to use block grant funds over an array of generic services. Many sponsors were local governments who used CETA slots to fund municipal jobs. Program content varied among prime sponsors. CETA programs focused more on actual work experience rather than intensive training. In the decade of the 1970s, CETA's emphasis shifted from the disadvantaged or structurally unemployed to more skilled workers who had lost jobs due to the recession.

In 1974, the recession and the counter-cyclical forces caused Congress to enact Title VI, which authorized CETA funds to create jobs for the unemployed in state and local governments and in non-profit organizations. Public Service Employment (PSE) provided visible and useful services to communities and fiscal relief to hard-pressed cities. PSE was the nemesis of the program and created problems of inadequate participation by persons with lower socioeconomic status and the substitution of PSE to supplant rather than supplement local resources. Program abuses included (a) in pursuit of numbers, ineligible persons were enrolled; (b) programs were approved on the basis of expediency rather than usefulness; and (c) programs were not adequately monitored.

Congress responded with the Emergency Jobs Program Extension Act (EJPE) of 1976 and the Reauthorization Act of 1978. The Emergency Jobs Program Extension Act (EJPE) of 1976 extended Title VI, attempted to get the CETA program back on its original course, and sought to increase the number of disadvantaged persons in PSE programs. The Reauthorization Act of 1978 had more stringent requirements and self-enforcing devices. The reauthorization tightened the PSE by tightening entry requirements, restricting the wage levels, limiting the length of time a person could remain in PSE to 18 months, requiring that employability development plans be prepared for all Title II participants, and requiring that a job training component be added to PSE jobs. It stipulated rigorous procedures for determining and verifying the eligibility of CETA applicants, held prime sponsors liable for improper enrollments, and imposed stronger monitoring measures.

The Comprehensive Employment and Training Act (CETA) did not improve the labor market performance of its clients but provided significant amounts of employment to the otherwise unemployed. It also augmented the labor supply available to local and state governments and made possible increased public services.

Job Training Partnership Act (JTPA) The most recent manpower training program is the Job Training Partnership Act (JTPA). This law, enacted in 1982, authorizes a series of employment and training programs for various target groups. The largest program, under Title IIA of the Act, provides block grants to the states for the administration of employment and training services for economically disadvantaged youth, adults, and long-term unemployed persons. The states are responsible for allocating funds, by formula, to cities and counties with populations of 200,000 or more, known as service delivery areas (SDAs). Funds are appropriated on a Program Year (PY) basis, i.e., July 1 - June 30.

Under Title IIA of JTPA, programs are administered in service delivery areas under a public-private partnership arrangement. Locally elected officials appoint Private Industry Councils (PIC) to plan and oversee local programs. The majority of the PIC members represent business and industry. The remaining members represent other sectors of the community, including education, labor, community-based organizations, the Employment Service, and vocational rehabilitation, and economic development agencies.

Services under the Department of Labor's JTPA program are not limited to job training but also include basic skills and remedial education, counseling, and job placement assistance. The goal of the Act is to move the jobless into permanent and unsubsidized, self-sustaining employment. These programs are usually augmented by supportive services such as child care and transportation.

Expert Panel Review Letter

Month and Day, 1995

Name
Title
Organization
Street Address
City, State and Zip

Dear Name:

Thank you for agreeing to review my survey instrument for content validity. As I explained when I called, I am a faculty member at the University of Massachusetts at Amherst. I am currently conducting a study to determine the important components of education and employment training programs in transitional settings for homeless women with children. I have undertaken this study (1) to determine what are the components of current transitional programs for homeless women with children and (2) to determine the importance of each program component in a comprehensive transitional program that assists homeless women with children to become self-sufficient. I will be conducting a national survey of homeless transitional shelters and transitional housing programs for women with children.

I am asking you to review the enclosed proposed questionnaire. Comments can be written directly on the questionnaire. Please comment on :

1. Clarity and appropriateness of directions and title of the survey. .

2. Completeness of the content of program components, program outcomes, and program and client profile questions. Are there any that should be added or deleted? Please note additions or deletions on the questionnaire.

3. Clarity of statements.

4. Appropriateness of scales and concepts to accomplish the purpose of the instrument.

5. Comment on the layout of the instrument. If the layout is a problem, what would you suggest?

6. Length of the instrument.

Please return the questionnaire with constructive comments in the enclosed, pre-stamped, pre-addressed envelope or fax me at (xxx) xxx-xxxx. If you have any questions please call me at (xxx) xxx-xxxx-Home or (xxx) xxx-xxxx-Office. I value the time, effort, and expertise required to provide the important information for the successful completion of the study. I would ask you to return the proposed questionnaire and comments by August 14, 1995. I appreciate your participation in the study, and anticipate the immediate return of the proposed questionnaire and comments. Thank you for your participation.

Sincerely,

Judy Kay Flohr, MS., RD.
Lecturer

Pretest Cover Letter

September 18, 1995

Name
Title
Organization
Street Address
City, State and Zip

Dear Name:

Thank you for agreeing to pre-test my survey instrument. I am a faculty member at the University of Massachusetts at Amherst. I am currently conducting a study to determine the education and employment training components in transitional programs for homeless women with children. I have undertaken this study (1) to determine what are the components of current transitional programs for homeless women with children and (2) to determine the importance of each program component in transitional programs that assist homeless women with children become self-sufficient. I will be conducting a national survey of homeless transitional shelters and transitional housing programs that serve homeless women with children.

I am asking you to complete the enclosed questionnaire and return the questionnaire in the enclosed, pre-stamped, pre-addressed envelope. I value your time and have tried to limit the effort required by you to provide the important information I require for the successful completion of the study. Would you please time how long it takes you *to complete the* questionnaire, comment on length, question content , clarity of directions and statements. Note any comments on the questionnaire. Please return the questionnaire by October 4, 1995. If you have any questions, please call me at (xxx) xxx-xxxx.

Your answers will be treated confidentially. No information will be presented or published in any way that would permit identification of any individual or organization. Your informed consent to participate in the pre-test under the conditions described is assumed by your completing the questionnaire and submitting it to the researcher. Do not complete the questionnaire of return it if you do not understand or agree to these conditions.

I appreciate your participation in the pre-test, and anticipate the immediate return of the questionnaire. Thank you for your participation.

Sincerely,

Judy Kay Flohr, MS., RD.
Instructor

Survey Cover Letter

Month and Date, 1995

Name
Title
Organization
Street Address
City, State and Zip

Dear Name:

Thank-you for agreeing to participate in my study. I am a faculty member at the University of Massachusetts at Amherst. I am currently conducting a study to determine the important components of education and job training programs in transitional settings for homeless women with children. I have undertaken this study to determine what program models that will help homeless women with children become self-sufficient. This survey provides an opportunity to have your views reflected.

I am asking you to complete the enclosed questionnaire and return the questionnaire in the enclosed, pre-stamped, pre-addressed envelope. I value your time and have tried to limit the effort required by you to provide the important information I require for the successful completion of the study. The questionnaire will require only 1 hour to complete. If you have any questions , call me at (xxx) xxx-xxxx. **Please return the questionnaire by November 13, 1995.**

Your answers will be treated confidentially and presented in statistical form only. No information will be presented or published in any way that would permit identification of any individual. There is an ID number on the questionnaire so I know that a questionnaire has been returned and no further reminder is needed. However, names will not be associated with the returns, and the list of sampled names will be destroyed as soon as data collection is complete.

Your informed consent to participate in the study under the conditions described is assumed by your completing the questionnaire and submitting it to the researcher. Do not complete the questionnaire of return it if you do not understand or agree to these conditions.

I appreciate your participation in the study, and anticipate the immediate return of the questionnaire. Thank you for your participation.

Sincerely,

Judy Kay Flohr, MS., RD.
Instructor

Survey Questionnaire

SURVEY ON EDUCATION AND EMPLOYMENT TRAINING COMPONENTS IN TRANSITIONAL PROGRAMS FOR HOMELESS WOMEN WITH CHILDREN

Study Purpose:

The purpose of this survey is to identify educational and employment training components in transitional programs for homeless women with children, and to determine program models which assists homeless women with children to become self-sufficient.

Questionnaire Sections:

Section I: Defines the survey population.

Section II: Defines major and minor program components in current transitional programs and evaluates each components' importance in a transitional program for homeless women with children. Each question table is a major component area. The major components include: Adult Basic Education; Family and Independent Living Skills Education; Employment Training; Children's Programs; Family Health and Preservation; Cultural, Recreational and Social Activities; Permanent Housing Assistance; and Case Management and Support Services.

Section III: Evaluates the current transitional program outcomes.

Section IV: Profiles your transitional program.

Section V: Profiles the participants of your transitional program, specifically women with children.

Please mark your responses clearly in the space provided. In categories where your choice is "Other: (Please Specify)_____", please write your choice in the space provided.

Unless otherwise indicated, answer all questions for current participants in your program who are women with children.

CONFIDENTIALITY: No information shall be presented or published in any way that would permit identification of any individual or organization.

RESEARCHER: Judy Kay Flohr
     Instructor and Doctoral Candidate
     University of Massachusetts at Amherst
     Box 32710 Flint Lab
     Amherst, MA 01003

SECTION I: SURVEY POPULATION DEFINITION

1. Does your transitional program provide services for homeless women with children?
      _____ Yes _____ No

If question #1 is answered no, please stop at this point and return the questionnaire in the envelope provided. If the answer to question #1 is yes, please continue with the survey.

SECTION II: PROGRAM COMPONENTS AND COMPONENT IMPORTANCE IN TRANSITIONAL PROGRAMS

If the answer to question A below is *YES* complete questions B and C. *In all events answer question D.*

In Question D indicate the importance of each program component in a transitional program for homeless women with children.
(Answer the question on each component whether you have the component or not.)

Adult Basic Education	A. Which program components are available to your participants? (Check one.)		B. IF YES, where is the component provided? (Check one.)			C. IF YES, who provides the component? (Check one.)		
PROGRAM COMPONENTS	Yes	No	On-Site	Off-Site	Both	Program Staff	Community Based Agency	Both
2. Adult Basic Education								
3. Individualized Education Plan (IEP)								
4. English as a Second Language (ESL)								
5. Literacy Education								
6. Math Skills								
7. GED Preparation								
8. Computer Applications/ Word Processing								
9. College Preparatory Guidance								
10. Other: _____								

D. In a transitional program for homeless women with children, evaluate the importance of each program component, *WHETHER PRESENTLY AVAILABLE TO PARTICIPANTS OR NOT.* (Circle the number which best describes its importance.)

Adult Basic Education

PROGRAM COMPONENTS	Not Important	Somewhat Important	Important	Very Important	Extremely Important
2. Adult Basic Education	1	2	3	4	5
3. Individualized Education Plan (IEP)	1	2	3	4	5
4. English as a Second Language (ESL)	1	2	3	4	5
5. Literacy Education	1	2	3	4	5
6. Math Skills	1	2	3	4	5
7. GED Preparation	1	2	3	4	5
8. Computer Applications/ Word Processing	1	2	3	4	5
9. College Preparatory Guidance	1	2	3	4	5
10. Other:_____	1	2	3	4	5

11. If adult basic education is a component of your program, where is this educational experience provided? (Check all that apply.)

_____ At Shelter Alternative High School (Board of Education)

_____ At Shelter Adult Education Program (Non-Board of Education)

_____ Public High School

_____ Vocational High School

_____ Community College

_____ Other (Please Specify) _____

If your program has an employment training component, please answer the following questions.

Family and Independent Living Skills Education

PROGRAM COMPONENTS	A. Which program components are available to your participants? (Check one.)		B. IF YES, where is the component provided? (Check one.)			C. IF YES, who provides the component? (Check one.)		
	Yes	No	On-Site	Off-Site	Both	Program Staff	Community Based Agency	Both
12. Family and Independent Living Skills Education								
13. Parenting								
14. Child Development and Behavior Management								
15. Child Abuse Awareness								
16. Housing and Independent Living								
17. Budgeting and Money Management								
18. Credit /Debt Management								
19. Time Management								
20. Health and Hygiene								

Family and Independent Living Skills Education

PROGRAM COMPONENTS	A. Which program components are available to your participants? (Check one.)		B. IF YES, where is the component provided? (Check one.)			C. IF YES, who provides the component? (Check one.)		
	Yes	No	On-Site	Off-Site	Both	Program Staff	Community Based Agency	Both
21. Nutrition								
22. Stress Management								
23. AIDS/HIV and STD Awareness								
24. Domestic Violence Awareness								
25. Self-Esteem, Motivation and Attitude Development								
26. Use of Community Resources								
27. Legal Issues								
28. Other: (Please Specify)								

D. In a transitional program for homeless women with children, evaluate the importance of each program component, *WHETHER PRESENTLY AVAILABLE OR NOT.* (Circle the number which best describes its importance.)

Family and Independent Living Skills Education

PROGRAM COMPONENTS	Not Important	Somewhat Important	Important	Very Important	Extremely Important
12. Family and Independent Living Skills Education	1	2	3	4	5
13. Parenting	1	2	3	4	5
14. Child Development and Behavior Management	1	2	3	4	5
15. Child Abuse Awareness	1	2	3	4	5
16. Housing and Independent Living	1	2	3	4	5
17. Budgeting and Money Management	1	2	3	4	5
18. Credit /Debt Management	1	2	3	4	5
19. Time Management	1	2	3	4	5
20. Health and Hygiene	1	2	3	4	5

Family and Independent Living Skills Education					
D. In a transitional program for homeless women with children, evaluate the importance of each program component, *WHETHER PRESENTLY AVAILABLE OR NOT.* (Circle the number which best describes its importance.)					
PROGRAM COMPONENTS	Not Important	Somewhat Important	Important	Very Important	Extremely Important
21. Nutrition	1	2	3	4	5
22. Stress Management	1	2	3	4	5
23. AIDS/HIV and STD Awareness	1	2	3	4	5
24. Domestic Violence Awareness	1	2	3	4	5
25. Self-Esteem, Motivation and Attitude Development	1	2	3	4	5
26. Use of Community Resources	1	2	3	4	5
27. Legal Issues	1	2	3	4	5
28. Other: (Please Specify)	1	2	3	4	5

Employment Training

PROGRAM COMPONENTS	A. Which program components are available to your participants? (Check one.)		B. IF YES, where is the component provided? (Check one.)			C. IF YES, who provides the component? (Check one.)		
	Yes	No	On-Site	Off-Site	Both	Program Staff	Community Based Agency	Both
29. Employment Training								
30. Indv. Vocational Plan								
31. Occupational Exploration								
32. Employability and Skills Assessments								
33. Job Search Assistance/ Job Search Preparatory Training								
34. Job Readiness/ Pre-Employment Training								
35. Vocational and Occupational Skills Training								
36. Entrepreneurial Training								
37. Job Placement								
38. Other: (Please Specify)								

D. In a transitional program for homeless women with children, evaluate the importance of each program component, *WHETHER PRESENTLY AVAILABLE OR NOT.* (Circle the number which best describes its importance.)

Employment Training

PROGRAM COMPONENTS	Not Important	Somewhat Important	Important	Very Important	Extremely Important
29. Employment Training	1	2	3	4	5
30. Indv. Vocational Plan	1	2	3	4	5
31. Occupational Exploration	1	2	3	4	5
32. Employability and Skills Assessments	1	2	3	4	5
33. Job Search Assistance/ Job Search Preparatory Training	1	2	3	4	5
34. Job Readiness/ Pre-Employment Training	1	2	3	4	5
35. Vocational and Occupational Skills Training	1	2	3	4	5
36. Entrepreneurial Training	1	2	3	4	5
37. Job Placement	1	2	3	4	5
38. Other: (Please Specify)	1	2	3	4	5

39. What types of employment training are available to your
participants? (Check all that apply.)

_____ Vocational/Occupational Skills Training

_____ Paid Internships

_____ Mentoring Internships

_____ On-The-Job Train

_____ Apprenticeship Program

_____ Work Experience/Transitional Employment Placements

_____ Other (Please Specify) _____

40. Where is this employment training provided? (Check all that apply.)

_____ Vocational School

_____ Vocational Center

_____ Community College/Post-Secondary Institution

_____ JTPA Training Program

_____ State Welfare to Work Program

_____ Community College Vocational Training Center

_____ Sheltered Workshop

_____ On Site

_____ Other (Please Specify) _____

41. How many hours per week is the average woman participant
involved in employment training? (Check one.)

_____ Less that 10 hours

_____ 10-20 hours

_____ 21-30 hours

_____31-40 hours

_____ over 40 hours

42. How do you provide job placement services? (Check all that apply.)

_____ Vendor/contractors/and organizations

_____ Job Banks

_____ Job Service/Employment Service

_____ Newspaper

_____ Self Directed Job Search

_____ Other (Please Specify) _____

Children's Programs

PROGRAM COMPONENTS	A. Which program components are available to your participants? (Check one.)		B. IF YES, where is each component provided? (Check one.)			C. IF YES, who provides the component? (Check one.)		
	Yes	No	On-Site	Off-Site	Both	Program Staff	Community Based Agency	Both
43. Children's Programs								
44. Preschool and Child Care Programs								
45. After School Programs								
46. Counseling								
47. Activities during parent meetings								
48. Art/Play Therapy								
49. Other: (Please Specify)								

Children's Programs

D. In a transitional program for homeless women with children, evaluate the importance of each program component, *WHETHER PRESENTLY AVAILABLE OR NOT.* (Circle the number which best describes its importance.)

PROGRAM COMPONENTS	Not Important	Somewhat Important	Important	Very Important	Extremely Important
43. Children's Programs	1	2	3	4	5
44. Preschool and Child Care Programs	1	2	3	4	5
45. After School Programs	1	2	3	4	5
46. Counseling	1	2	3	4	5
47. Activities during parent meetings	1	2	3	4	5
48. Art/Play Therapy	1	2	3	4	5
49. Other: (Please Specify)	1	2	3	4	5

Cultural, Recreational, and Social Activities (Women and Children)	A. Which program components are available to your participants? (Check one.)		B. IF YES, where is the component provided? (Check one.)			C. IF YES, who provides the component? (Check one.)		
PROGRAM COMPONENTS	Yes	No	On-Site	Off-Site	Both	Program Staff	Community Based Agency	Both
50. Cultural, Recreational and Social Activities								

Cultural, Recreational, and Social Activities (Women and Children)	D. In a transitional program for homeless women with children, evaluate the importance of each program component, *WHETHER PRESENTLY AVAILABLE OR NOT.* (Circle the number which best describes its importance.)				
PROGRAM COMPONENTS	Not Important	Somewhat Important	Important	Very Important	Extremely Important
50. Cultural, Recreational and Social Activities	1	2	3	4	5

Family Health and Preservation	A. Which program components are available to your participants? (Check one.)		B. IF YES, where is the component provided? (Check one.)			C. IF YES, who provides each component? (Check one.)		
PROGRAM COMPONENTS	Yes	No	On-Site	Off-Site	Both	Program Staff	Community Based Agency	Both
51. Family Health and Preservation								
52. Health Services								
53. Individual/Family Counseling								
54. Substance Abuse Assessment								
55. Substance Abuse Treatment								
56. Substance Abuse Counseling								
57. Mentoring /Peer Support Groups								
58. Foster Care Prevention								
59. Family Reunification								
60. Other: (Please Specify) ___								

Family Health and Preservation

D. In a transitional program for homeless women with children, evaluate the importance of each program component, *WHETHER PRESENTLY AVAILABLE OR NOT.* (Circle the number which best describes its importance.)

PROGRAM COMPONENTS	Not Important	Somewhat Important	Important	Very Important	Extremely Important
51. Family Health and Preservation	1	2	3	4	5
52. Health Services	1	2	3	4	5
53. Individual/Family Counseling	1	2	3	4	5
54. Substance Abuse Assessment	1	2	3	4	5
55. Substance Abuse Treatment	1	2	3	4	5
56. Substance Abuse Counseling	1	2	3	4	5
57. Mentoring/Peer Support Groups	1	2	3	4	5
58. Foster Care Prevention	1	2	3	4	5
59. Family Reunification	1	2	3	4	5
60. Other: (Please Specify)	1	2	3	4	5

Permanent Housing Assistance	A. Which program components are available to your participants? (Check one.)		B. IF YES, where is the component provided? (Check one.)			C. IF YES, who provides the component? (Check one.)		
PROGRAM COMPONENTS	Yes	No	On-Site	Off-Site	Both	Program Staff	Community Based Agency	Both
61. Permanent Housing Assistance								
62. House Search/Location Assistance								
63. Entitlement Assistance								
64. Housing Advocacy								
65. Other: (Please Specify)								

Permanent Housing Assistance	D. In a transitional program for homeless women with children, evaluate the importance of each program component, *WHETHER PRESENTLY AVAILABLE OR NOT*. (Circle the number which best describes its importance.)				
PROGRAM COMPONENTS	Not Important	Somewhat Important	Important	Very Important	Extremely Important
61. Permanent Housing Assistance	1	2	3	4	5
62. House Search/Location Assistance	1	2	3	4	5
63. Entitlement Assistance	1	2	3	4	5
64. Housing Advocacy	1	2	3	4	5
65. Other: (Please Specify)	1	2	3	4	5

Case Management and Support Services (Cont.) During and after Program Completion	A. Which program components are available to your participants?(Check one.)		B. IF YES, when is the component provided? (Check one.)			C. IF YES, who provides the component? (Check one.)		
PROGRAM COMPONENTS	Yes	No	On-Site	Off-Site	Both	Program Staff	Community Based Agency	Both
66. Case Management								
67. Needs Assessment								
68. Service Plan								
69. Coordination of Services								
70. Support Services								
71. Follow-up: Housing								
72. Follow-up: Education								

Case Management and Support Services (Cont.) During and after Program Completion. PROGRAM COMPONENTS	D. In a transitional program for homeless women with children, evaluate the importance of each program component, *WHETHER PRESENTLY AVAILABLE OR NOT.* (Circle the number which best describes its importance.)				
	Not Important	Somewhat Important	Important	Very Important	Extremely Important
66. Case Management	1	2	3	4	5
67. Needs Assessment	1	2	3	4	5
68. Service Plan	1	2	3	4	5
69. Coordination of Services	1	2	3	4	5
70. Support Services	1	2	3	4	5
71. Follow-up: Housing	1	2	3	4	5
72. Follow-up: Education	1	2	3	4	5

Case Management and Support Services (Cont.) During and after Program Completion	A. Which program components are available to your participants?(Check one.)		B. IF YES, when is the component provided? (Check one.)			C. IF YES, who provides the component? (Check one.)		
PROGRAM COMPONENTS	Yes	No	On-Site	Off-Site	Both	Program Staff	Community Based Agency	Both
73. Follow-up: Employment								
74. Follow-up: Mental/Physical Health Issues								
75. Transportation Assistance								
76. Child Care Assistance								
77. Clothing/Work Equipment Assistance								
78. Legal Assistance								
79. Financial Counseling								
80. Other: (Please Specify)								

Case Management and Support Services (Cont.) During and after Program Completion	D. In a transitional program for homeless women with children, evaluate the importance of each program component, *WHETHER PRESENTLY AVAILABLE OR NOT.* (Circle the number which best describes its importance.)				
PROGRAM COMPONENTS	Not Important	Somewhat Important	Important	Very Important	Extremely Important
73. Follow- up: Employment	1	2	3	4	5
74. Follow-up: Mental/Physical Health Issues	1	2	3	4	5
75. Transportation Assistance	1	2	3	4	5
76. Child Care Assistance	1	2	3	4	5
77. Clothing/Work Equipment Assistance	1	2	3	4	5
78. Legal Assistance	1	2	3	4	5
79. Financial Counseling	1	2	3	4	5
80. Other: (Please Specify)	1	2	3	4	5

81. What type of follow-up services are provided after program completion? (Check all that apply.)

_____ Phone call

_____ Home Visit

_____ Employer Visit

_____ Mailings

_____ Case Management Services

_____ Support Groups

_____Other: (Please specify) _____

82. What is the length of the follow-up after program completion? (Check one.)

_____ Less than 1 Day

_____1 Day

_____ 1 Week

_____ 1 Month

_____ 3 Months

_____6 months

_____ 1 Year

_____ Over 1 Year

83. How is the follow-up funded?   (Check one.)

[ ] Fully Funded

[ ] Partially Funded

[ ] Not Funded

84. How many employee hours per week are spent in follow-up after program completion? (Please specify the number of hours per week.)

_____ Hours Per Week

SECTION III: EVALUATION OF PROGRAM OUTCOMES

85. Upon completion of your program, what percentage of your participants who are women with children increased their educational level? (Check one.)

_____ Less that 20%

_____ 21- 40%

_____41-60%

_____ 61-80%

_____ over 80%

86. Upon completion of your program, what percentage of your participants who are women with children increased their residential stability? (Check one.)

_____ Less that 20%
_____ 21- 40%
_____41-60%
_____ 61-80%
_____ over 80%

87. Upon completion of your program, what percentage of your participants who are women with children improved their employment status? (Check one.)

_____ Less that 20%
_____ 21- 40%
_____41-60%
_____ 61-80%
_____ over 80%

88. Upon completion of your program, what percentage of your participants who are women with children increased their income? (Check one.)

_____ Less that 20%
_____ 21- 40%
_____41-60%
_____ 61-80%
_____ over 80%

SECTION IV: PROGRAM PROFILES

89. Which best describes your transitional program? (Check one.)
    [ ] Transitional Shelter
    [ ] Emergency and Transitional Shelter
    [ ] Domestic Violence Shelter
    [ ] Transitional Housing/Living Program
    [ ] Other (Please Specify) _____

90. How many transitional units does your program have? (Check one.)
    [ ] Less than 5 units
    [ ] 5-10 units
    [ ] 11-15 units
    [ ] 16-20 units
    [ ] 21-25 units
    [ ] Over 25 unit

91. What is the length of your transitional program? (Check one.)
    [ ] 1-6 months
    [ ] 7-12 months
    [ ] 13-18 months
    [ ] 19-24 months
    [ ] Over 24 months

92. What is the *ideal length* of a transitional program based on the needs of the homeless women with children you are serving? (Check one.)
    [ ] 1-6 months
    [ ] 7-12 months
    [ ] 13-18 months
    [ ] 19-24 months
    [ ] Over 24 months

93. Which of the following agencies have linkages with your program (e.g., accept referrals, refer to, provide services)? (Check all that apply.)
    _____ Housing providers
    _____ Educational Institutions/Providers
    _____ Job Training Providers/Vocational Centers
    _____ Job Service/Employment Service
    _____ JTPA Private Industry Council
    _____ Welfare Agencies
    _____ Community Social Service Agencies
    _____ State Cooperative Extension
    _____ Businesses
    _____ Non-Profit/Secular Organizations
    _____ Non-Profit/ Religious Organizations
    _____ Community Advocates
    _____ Mental Health Organizations
    _____ Welfare to Work Program
    _____ Other: (Please Specify) _____

94. Rank your sources of funding according to the following scale. (Write the number corresponding to your answer in the space provided.)

(1) Most Important Funding Source; (2) Important Funding Source; (3) Less Important Funding Source; (4) Not a Funding Source

Rank	*Funding Source*
_____	Supportive Housing Program's (SHP) Transitional Housing Program (HUD Program)
_____	Title IIA of The Job Training Partnership Act (JTPA)
_____	Community Services Block Grant (CSBG)
_____	Carl D. Perkins Vocational Education Act
_____	Federal Anti-Drug Funds
_____	Other Federal Government Program: (Please Specify)

_____

_____	State Government Funds
_____	Local Government Funds
_____	Private Sector Organization(s) (e.g., Corporations)
_____	Non-Profit Organization(s)/Secular
_____	Non-Profit Organization(s)/ Religious Affiliation
_____	Foundation(s)
_____	United Way
_____	Private Contributions
_____	Other: (Please Specify)

_____

SECTION V: CLIENT PROFILE

95. How many of the following are currently participating your transitional program? (List total number of each type of participant.)

_____ Women with Children
_____ Intact Families
_____ Men with Children
_____ Single Men
_____ Single Women

PLEASE ANSWER THE FOLLOWING QUESTIONS ONLY ON
PARTICIPANTS WHO ARE *WOMEN WITH CHILDREN.*

96. What is the age distribution of your program's women participants?
(List total number of participants in each age category.)

_____ Under 15
_____ 15-19
_____ 20-24
_____ 25-29
_____ 30-34
_____ 35-39
_____ 40 and over

97. What is the race or ethnic origin of your program's women
participants? (List total number of participants in each race or ethnic
origin category.)

_____ White (not Hispanic)
_____ Black (not Hispanic)
_____ Hispanic
_____ Asian or Pacific Islander
_____ American Indian/Alaska Native
_____ Other

98. What is the marital status of your program's women participants?
(List total number of participants in each marital status category.)

_____ Single (Never married)
_____ Married
_____ Separated
_____ Divorced
_____ Widowed

99. What is the average number of children in each family? (Check
one.)

[ ] 1
[ ] 2
[ ] 3
[ ] 4
[ ] 5
[ ] 6
[ ]Over 6

100. What is the age of the children in your program? (List total number of children in each age category.)

_____ 0-2 years old

_____ 3-5 years old

_____ 6-11 years old

_____ 12-18 years old

101. At what frequency do the following factors lead to your women participants' homelessness. (Circle the number that best describe the factors frequency.)

(1) Most Frequent Factor; (2) More Frequent Factor; (3) Frequent Factor; (4) Less Frequent Factor; (5)Not a Factor

A. Housing Condemned/Sold/Converted

| 1 | 2 | 3 | 4 | 5 |

B. Evicted, Unable to Pay Rent

| 1 | 2 | 3 | 4 | 5 |

C. Lack of Affordable Housing

| 1 | 2 | 3 | 4 | 5 |

D. Relocated for Improved Job Market

| 1 | 2 | 3 | 4 | 5 |

E. Lost Job/Lack of Employment Opportunities

| 1 | 2 | 3 | 4 | 5 |

F. Termination of Public Assistance

| 1 | 2 | 3 | 4 | 5 |

G. Release from Prison

| 1 | 2 | 3 | 4 | 5 |

H. Release from Mental Health Institution

| 1 | 2 | 3 | 4 | 5 |

I. Release from Substance Abuse Treatment

| 1 | 2 | 3 | 4 | 5 |

J. Chronic Alcohol Use

| 1 | 2 | 3 | 4 | 5 |

K. Chronic Drug Use

| 1 | 2 | 3 | 4 | 5 |

L.   Mental Illness
1   2   3   4   5

M. Physical Disability
1   2   3   4   5

N. Illness—Family or Personal
1   2   3   4   5

O. Physical Abuse/Sexual Abuse/Domestic Violence
1   2   3   4   5

Q. Divorce/Termination of Personal Relationship
1   2   3   4   5

R.   Family Threw Them Out
1   2   3   4   5

S.   Runaway/Transient
1   2   3   4   5

T.   Other: (Please Specify) _____
1   2   3   4   5

102. What is the educational attainment distribution of the program's
women participants? (List the total number of participants in each
educational attainment category.)

_____ Grade School (0-7)
_____ Some High School (8-11)
_____ High School Graduate (12) or GED
_____ Some Vocational Technical School
_____ Vocational Technical School Graduate
_____ Some College (13-15)
_____ College Graduate (16)
_____ Graduate School (16+)

103. What was the employment history of your women participants
before program participation? (List total number of participants in each
employment category.)

_____ Employed Full-Time
_____ Employed Part-Time
_____ Employed Sporadically
_____ Unemployed/Looking for Work

_____ Unemployed/Not Looking for Work
_____ Disabled/Incapable of Work
_____ Never Employed
_____ Other: (Please Specify) _____

104. What is your assessment of the employability of your women participants? (List total number of participants in each employability category.)
_____ Definitely Not Employable
_____ Probably Not Employable
_____ Probably Employable
_____ Definitely Employable

105. How accountable are the following factors for your women participants' lack of employability. (Circle the number that best describs the factors accountability.)

(1) Most Accountable Factor (2) More Accountable Factor; (3)Accountable Factor; (4) Less Accountable Factor; (5) Not an Accountable Factor

A. Physical Disability
1   2   3   4   5

B. Mental, Psychiatric Impairment
1   2   3   4   5

C. Alcohol Abuse
1   2   3   4   5

D. Drug Abuse
1   2   3   4   5

E. Discharge from Institution
1   2   3   4   5

F. Lack of Education
1   2   3   4   5

G. Lack of Competitive Employment Skills
1   2   3   4   5

H. Lack of Employment Opportunities
1   2   3   4   5

I. Lack of Interpersonal Skills
1   2   3   4   5

J. Communication Problems
1   2   3   4   5

K. Lack of Grooming
1   2   3   4   5

L. Lack of Child Care
1   2   3   4   5

M. Lack of Transportation
1   2   3   4   5

O. Age (Too Young)
1   2   3   4   5

P. Other: (Please Specify) _____
1   2   3   4   5

THANK YOU VERY MUCH FOR PARTICIPATING.

Please return in included envelope to:

Judy Kay Flohr
HRTA Department
Box 32710 Flint Lab
University of Massachusetts at Amherst
Amherst, MA 01003

Should you have questions, please contact me at (413) 545-4042.
If you would like a summary of the survey's results please fill in the
following and mail it to me at the above address.

Name: _____
Address: _____
             _____

Reminder Postcard

Judy Kay Flohr
University of Massachusetts Amherst
Amherst, MA 01003
Month and Date, 1995

Dear Survey Participant:

Three weeks ago I mailed you a questionnaire about components of transitional programs that serve homeless women with children. I am writing again to stress how important it is that you complete the questionnaire. I need you to participant in order that the study accurately determines the important components in transitional programs that serve homeless women with children. If you have already completed and returned the questionnaire, I thank you. If not, please complete the questionnaire and return it. Should you need another questionnaire call me at (xxx) xxx-xxxx. **Thank you for your participation.**

Sincerely,

Judy Kay Flohr
Instructor

Reminder Postcard

Bibliography

Adler, W. C. (1991). *Addressing homelessness: Status of programs under the Stewart B. McKinney homeless assistance act and related legislation.* Washington, DC: National Governors' Association.

Adler, W., & Lederer, J. (1991). Barriers, real and imagined: Providing job training for the homeless through JTPA, in *Labor notes: Homeless in America: Self- sufficiency through employment and training programs,* National Governors' Association, Center for Policy Research, (June, 1991), 7.

American Academy of Political and Social Science. (1989). *The ghetto underclass: Social science perspectives.* Newbury Park, NY: Sage Publications.

Axelson, L. J., & Dail, P. W. (1988). The changing character of homelessness in the United States. *Family Relations, 37,* 463-469.

Bachrach, L. L. (1987). Homeless women: A context for health planning. *The Milbank Quarterly, 65,* 371-396.

Bahr, H. M., & Garrett G. R. (1976). *Women alone: The disaffiliation of urban females.* Lexington, MA: Lexington Books.

Baker, S. G. (1994). Gender, ethnicity, and homelessness. *American Behavioral Scientist, 37*(4), 476-504.

Bassuk, E. L., & Buckner, J. C. (1994). Troubling families: A commentary. *American Behavioral Scientist, 37*(3), 412-421.

Bassuk, E. L., Carman, R. W., Weinreb, L. F., & Herzig, M. M. (1991). *Community Care for homeless families: A program design manual.* Newton, MA: Better Homes and Gardens Foundation.

Bassuk, E. L., & Rosenberg, L. (1988). Why does family homelessness occur? A case- control study. *American Journal of Public Health, 78,* 783-788.

Bassuk, E. L., & Rubin, L. (1987). Homeless children: A neglected population. *American Journal of Orthopsychiatry, 57,* 279-286.

Bassuk, E. L., Rubin, L., & Lauriat, A. S. (1986). The characteristics of sheltered homeless families. *American Journal of Public Health, 76,* 1097-1101.

Baum, A. S., & Burnes, D. W. (1993). *A nation in denial: The truth about homelessness.* Boulder, CO: Westview Press.

Baumohl, J. (1992). Hope needs work: Picking up from Hopper and Hawks. *British Journal of Addiction, 87,* 15-16.

Berlin, G., & McAllister, W. (1994). Homeless family shelters and family homelessness. *American Behavioral Scientist, 37(3),* 422-434.

Birch, E. L. (1985). *The unsheltered woman: Women and housing in the 80's.* New Brunswick, NJ: Rutgers Center for Urban Policy Research.

Blank, S., Collins, R., & Smith, S. (1992). *Pathways to self-sufficiency for two generations.* New York, NY: Foundation for Child Development.

Blau, J. (1992). *The visible poor: Homelessness in the United States.* New York, NY: Oxford University Press.

Borg, W. R., & Gall, M. D.(1989). *Educational research: An introduction (5th ed).* New York, NY: Longman.

Breakey, W. R., Fischer, P. J., Kramer, M., Nestadt, G., Romanoski, A. J., Ross, A., Royal, R. M., Stein, O. C. (1989). Health and mental health problems of homeless men and women in Baltimore. *Journal of the American Medical Association, 262,* 1352-1357.

Bulman, P. M. (1993). *Caught in the mix: An oral portrait of homelessness.* Westport, CT: Auburn House.

Burghardt, J., Rangarajan, A., Gordon, A., & Kisker, E. (1992). *Evaluation of the minority female single parent demonstration: Summary report.* New York, NY: The Rockefeller Foundation.

Burn, S. M. (1992). Loss of control, attributions, and helplessness in the homeless. *Journal of Applied Social Psychology, 22,* 1161-1174.

Burt, M. R. (1992). *The growth of homelessness in the 1980s.* New York, NY: Russell Sage Foundation & Washington, DC: Urban Institute Press.

Burt, M. R., & Cohen, B. E. (1989). *America's homeless: Numbers, characteristics, and the programs that serve them.* Washington, DC: Urban Institute Press.

Burt, M. R., & Cohen, B. E. (1989). Differences among homeless single women, women with children, and single men. *Social Problems, 36,* 508-524.

Center on Budget and Policy Priorities. (1993). *Poverty remains high in 1992 despite economic recovery.* Washington, DC: Center on Budget and Policy Priorities.

Center on Budget and Policy Priorities. (1995, March 23). *Proposed Changes to Federal Entitlement Programs.* Washington, DC: C-Span.

Clement, P. F. (1984). The transformation of the wandering poor in nineteenth-century Philadelphia. In E. H. Monkkonen (Ed.), *Walking to work: Tramps in America, 1790-1935.* (pp. 56-86) Lincoln, NE: University of Nebraska Press.

Crouse, J. M. (1986). *The homeless transient in the great depression: New York State 1929-1941.* Albany , NY: State University of New York Press.

Crystal, S. (1984). Homeless men and homeless women: The gender gap. *Urban and Social Change Review, 17,* 2-6.

DaCosta Nunez, R. (1994). *Hopes, dreams, & promise: The future of homeless children in America.* New York, NY: Institute for Children and Poverty.

Dail, P. W. (1990). The psychosocial context of homeless mothers with young children: Program and policy implications. *Child Welfare, 69,* 291-308.

Dakin, L. S. (1987). Homelessness: The role of the legal profession in finding solutions through litigation. *Family Law Quarterly, 21,* 93-123.

Davis, D., & Cosenza, R. (1985). *Business research for decision making.* Boston, MA: Kent Publishing Company.

Dillman, D. (1978). *Mail and telephone surveys: The total design method.* New York, NY: John Wiley & Sons.

Dornbusch, S. M. (1994). Additional perspectives on homeless families. *American Behavioral Scientist, 37*(3), 404-411.

Dunne, F. J. (1990). Alcohol abuse on skid row: In sight out of mind. *Alcohol & Alcoholism, 25,* 13-15.

Easterlin, R. A. (1987). The new age structure of poverty in America: Permanent or transient? *Population and Development Review, 13,* 195-208.

Filipczak, B., Geber, B., & Gordon, J. (1991, February). Days Inn hires the homeless. *Training Today,* 12-13.

First, R. J. (1990). *Preliminary findings on rural homelessness in Ohio.* (Report No. RC 017 937) Columbus: Ohio State University, Columbus College of Social Work. (ERIC Document Reproduction Service No. ED 326 374).

First, R. J., Roth, D., & Arewa, B. D. (1988). Homelessness: Understanding the dimensions of the problem for minorities. *Social Work, 33,* 120-124.

Flynn, R. L. (1986). *Making room: Comprehensive policy for the homeless.* Boston, MA: City of Boston.

Garfinklel, I., & McLanahan, S. S. (1986). *Single mothers and their children: A new American dilemma.* Washington, DC: The Urban Institute Press.

Gallagher, E. (1986). *No place like home: A report on the tragedy of homeless children and their families in Massachusetts.* Boston, MA: Massachusetts Committee For Children and Youth.

Garrett, G. R., and Bahr, H. M. (1973). *Skid row: An introduction to disaffiliation.* New York, NY: Oxford University Press.

Glasser, I. (1994). *Homelessness in global perspective.* New York, NY: G. K. Hall & Co.

Goering, P., Durbin, J., Trainor, J., & Paduchak, D. (1990). Developing housing for the homeless. *Psychological Rehabilitation Journal, 13,* 33-42.

Goering. P., Paduchak, D., & Durban, J. (1990). Housing homeless women: A consumer preference study. *Hospital and Community Psychiatry, 41,* 790-794.

Goldberg, G. S., & Kremen, E. (1987). The feminization of poverty: Only in America. *Social Policy, 17,* 3-14.

Golden, S. (1992). *The women outside: Meanings and myths of homelessness.* Berkeley, CA: University of California Press.

Goodman, L., Saxe, L., & Harvey, M. (1991). Homelessness as psychological trauma. *American Psychologist, 46,* 1219-1225.

Greenfield, M. (1993, November). When the burning stops. *Newsweek,* 102.

Greenwood, K. B. (Ed.), (1981). *Contemporary challenges for vocational education.* Alexandria, VA: American Vocational Association.

Greenwood, K. B. (1982). A historical look at the politics in vocational education. In R. A. Sievers (Ed.), *The politics of vocational education* (pp. 3-9). Alexandria, VA: American Vocational Association.

Guagenti-Tax, E., & Mulvihill, L. (1992). *Improved Work readiness, work attitudes, interpersonal relations, and work quality among substance abusers attending the New Leaf program.* (Report No. UD 028 912) Bronx, NY: Argus Community, Inc. (ERIC Document Reproduction Service No. ED 351 407).

Gueron, J. M., & Pauly, E. (1991). *From welfare to work.* New York, NY: Russell Sage Foundation.

Hagen, J. L. (1987). Gender and homelessness. *Social Work, 32,* 312-316.

Hagen, J. L. (1989). Participants in a day program for the homeless: A survey of characteristics and service needs. *Psychosocial Rehabilitation Journal, 12,* 29-37.

Hartman, A. (1989). Homelessness: Public issue and private trouble. *Social Work, 34,* 483-484.

Heard, D. R., & Boxhill, N. A. (1988). Two steps back, one step forward: Homeless women and their children at a transition house. *Sage, 5,* 50-51.

Hemminger, H., & Quinones, W. (1992). Let them have housing. In O'Malley, P. & Flynn, R. L. (Eds), *Homelessness, New England and Beyond* (pp. 557-581) Amherst: University of Massachusetts Press.

Heritage Foundation. (1988). *Rethinking policy on homelessness.* Washington, DC: Author

Hill, R. P. (1991). Homeless women, special possessions, and the meaning of "home": An ethnographic case study. *Journal of Consumer Research, 18,* 298-310.

Hirsch, K. (1989). *Songs from the alley.* New York, NY: Ticknor & Fields.

Hombs, E., & Snyder, M. (1986). *Homelessness in America: A forced march to nowhere.* Washington, DC: Community for Creative Non-violence.

Homes for the Homeless. (1996). *Common sense: Why jobs and training won't end welfare for the homeless families.* New York, NY: Author.

Homes for the Homeless. (1997). *For whom the bell tolls: The institutionalization of Homeless families in America .* New York, NY: Author.

Homes for the Homeless. (1996). *Day to day. . .parent to child: The future of violence among homeless children in America.* New York, NY: Author.

Hopper, K. (1988). More than passing strange: Homelessness and mental illness in New York City. *American Ethnologist, 15,* 155-167.

Hooper, K., & Baumohl, J. (1994). Held in abeyance: Rethinking homelessness and advocacy. *American Behavioral Scientist, 37*(4), 522-552.

Institute for Children and Poverty. (1994). *Job readiness: Crossing the threshold from homelessness to employment.* New York, NY: Institute for Children and Poverty.

Institute of Medicine. (1988). *Homelessness, health, and human needs.* Washington, DC: National Academy Press.

Jacobs, F. H. (1994). Defining a social problem: The case of family homelessness. *American Behavioral Scientist, 37*(3), 396-403.

Jencks, C. (1994). *The homeless.* Cambridge, MA: Harvard University Press.

Johnson, A. K. & Krueger, L. W. (1989). Toward a better understanding of homeless Women. *Social Work, 34,* 537-540.

Jones, D. L. (1984). The strolling poor: Transiency in eighteenth-century Massachusetts. In E. H. Monkkonen (Ed.), *Walking to work: Tramps in America, 1790-1935* (pp. 21-55). Lincoln, NE: University of Nebraska Press.

Kerlinger, F. N. (1986). *Foundations of behavioral research* (3rd ed). New York, NY: Horcourt Brace Jonvanovich College Publishers.

Kondratas, A. (1991). Ending homelessness. *American Psychologist, 46,* 1226-1231.

Koroloff, N. M., & Anderson, S. C. (1989). Alcohol-free living centers: Hope for homeless alcoholics. *Social Work, 34,* 497-504.

Kozol, J. (1988). *Rachel and her children.* New York, NY: Ballantine Books.

Lam, J. A. (1987). Homeless women in America: Their social and health characteristics (Doctoral dissertation, University of Massachusetts, 1987). Dissertation Abstracts International, 8805940.

Levitan, S. A., Gallo, F., & Shapiro, I. (1993). *Working but poor: America's contradiction.* Baltimore, MD: Johns Hopkins University Press.

Levitan, S. A., & Johnston, B. H. (1975). *The job corps: A social experiment that works.* Baltimore, MD: Johns Hopkins University Press.

Levitan, S. A., & Mangum, G. L. (1981). *The T in CETA: Local and national perspectives.* Kalamazoo, MI: W. E. Upjohn Institute for Employment Research.

Liebow, E. (1993). *Tell them who I am.* New York, NY: Macmillan.

Marin, P. (1987, January). Helping and hating the homeless. *Harpers,* 39-49.

Massachusetts State Department of Education. (1990). *Children without homes: A report by the Massachusetts Department of Education.* (Report No. UD 027 327). State Department of Education, Boston, MA. (ERIC Document Reproduction Service No. ED 316 629).

Massachusetts State Department of Education. (1991). *Faces of homelessness: A teacher's guide.* (Report No. CG 024 471) Quincy, MA: Office for the Education of Homeless Children and Youth. (ERIC Document Reproduction Service No. ED 348 641).

Maurin, J. T., Russell, L., & Memmott, R. J. (1989). An exploration of gender differences among the homeless. *Research in Nursing & Health, 12,* 315-321.

McBride, K. (1990). *Hope for the homeless.* (Report No. PS 018 790). Westchester, NY: The Child Care Council of Westchester. (ERIC Document Reproduction Service No. ED 319 507).

McCall, R. B. (1990). *Fundamental statistics for behavioral sciences,* (5th ed). New York, NY: Harcourt Brace Jovanovich.

McChesney, K. Y. (1987). *Mothers without: Homeless mothers and their children.* Unpublished dissertation, University of Southern California.

Milburn, N., & D'Ercole, A. (1991). Homeless women: Moving toward a comprehensive model. *American Psychologist, 46,* 1161-1169.

Miller, H. (1991). *On the fringe: The dispossessed in America.* Lexington, MA: Lexington Books.

Mills, C., & Ota, H. (1989). Homeless women with minor children in the Detroit metropolitan area. *Social Work, 34,* 485-489.

Mirengoff, W. (1981). The changing fortunes of CETA. In K. B. Greenwood (Ed.), *Contemporary Challenges for Vocational Education.* (pp. 85-95) Alexandria, VA: American Vocational Association.

Mitchell, J. C. (1987). The components of strong ties among homeless women. *Social Networks, 9,* 37-47.

Momeni, J. A. (1990). *Homelessness in the United States-Volume II: Data and issues.* New York, NY: Greenwood Press.

Monkkonen, E. H. 1984. *Walking to work in America, 1790-1935.* Lincoln, NE: University of Nebraska Press.

National Coalition for the Homeless. (1987). *Broken lives: Denial of education to homeless children.* Washington, DC: Author.

National Coalition for the Homeless. (1988a). *Necessary relief: The Stewart B. McKinney homeless assistance act.* Washington, DC: Author.

National Coalition for the Homeless. (1988b). *Over the edge: Homeless families and the welfare system.* Washington, DC: Author.

National Coalition for the Homeless. (1989). *Unfinished business: The Stewart B. McKinney homeless assistance act after two years.* Washington, DC: Author.

National Coalition for the Homeless. (1990a). *Summary of the Cranston-Gonzalez national affordable housing act.* Washington, DC: Author.

National Coalition for the Homeless. (1990b). *The closing door economic causes of homelessness.* Washington, DC: Author.

National Coalition for the Homeless. (1991). *Homelessness and the fiscal year 1992 federal budget.* Washington, DC: Author.

National Coalition for the Homeless. (1992a). *A place called hopelessness: Shelter demand in the 1990s.* Washington, DC: Author.

National Coalition for the Homeless. (1992b). *Addiction on the streets: Substance abuse and homelessness in America.* Washington, DC: Author.

National Coalition for the Homeless. (1992c). *Homelessness and the fiscal year 1993 federal budget.* Washington, DC: Author.

National Coalition for the Homeless. (1993). *Ending homelessness: A congressional briefing book.* Washington, DC: Author.

National Coalition for the Homeless. (1994). Congress goes home. *Safety Network, 13,* 5.

National Coalition for the Homeless (1997). *The McKinney Act.* Fact Sheet #18

National Coalition for the Homeless (1998) *Domestic Violence and Homelessness.* Fact Sheet #8

National Commission for Employment Policy. (1990). *Helping the homeless be choosers: The role of JTPA in improving job prospects.* (Special Report No. 28). Washington, DC.

New York State Education Department. (1990a). *Education for homeless adults: Strategies for implementation.* Albany, NY: Office of Workforce Preparation and Continuing Education.

New York State Education Department (1990b). *Literacy training for the homeless: Guidelines for effective programs.* Albany, NY: Bureau of Continuing Education Program Development.

New York State Education Department. (1990c) *The challenge in education: Meeting the needs of the homeless adult learner.* Albany, NY: Office of Continuing Education.

Norusis, J., & SPSS INC. (1994). *SPSS professional statistics 6.1.* Chicago, IL: SPSS Inc.

Norusis, J., & SPSS INC. (1993). SPSS for windows advanced statistics 6.0. Chicago, IL: SPSS Inc.

Norusis, J., & SPSS INC. (1993). *SPSS for windows base system users guide, release 6.0.* Chicago, IL: SPSS Inc.

Office of Policy Development and Research. (1995). *National evaluation of the supportive housing demonstration program.* Washington, DC: U.S. Department of Housing and Urban Development.

Office of Vocational and Adult Education. (1992). *Education for homeless adults: The 1989-1990 report.* Washington, DC: United States Department of Education.

O'Malley, P., & Flynn, R. L. (1992). *Homelessness, New England and beyond.* Amherst, MA: University of Massachusetts Press.

Patterson, K. J. (1984). Shelters and statistics: A new face to an old problem. *Urban and Social Change Review, 17,* 14-17.

Pearce, D. (1987). The feminization of poverty: Women, work and welfare. *Urban and Social Change Review, 17,* 28-35.

Relos, R., Ed. (1991). *North Carolina's homeless families: Issues for the 90s. Paper's from an invitational working conference.* (Report No. PS 019 753). Winston- Salem, NC: Babcock (Mary Reynolds) Foundation, Inc.; North Carolina State Department of Human Resources, Raleigh, NC. (ERIC Document Reproduction Service No. ED 336 187).

Ritchey, F. J., La Gory, M., Fitzpatrick, K. M., & Mullis, J. (1990). A comparison of homeless, community-wide, and selected distressed samples on the CES- depression scale. *American Journal of Public Health, 80,* 1384-1385.

Robertson, M. J. (1991). Homeless women with children. *American Psychologist, 46,* 1198-1204.

Rodgers, H. R. (1986). *Poor women, poor families.* Armonk, NY: M. E. Sharpe, Inc.

Rosenthal, R. (1994). *Homeless in paradise: A map of the terrain.* Philadelphia, PA: Temple University Press.

Rossi, P. H. (1989a). *Down and out in America: The origins of homelessness.* Chicago, IL: University of Chicago Press.

Rossi, P. H. (1989b). *Without shelter: Homelessness in the 1980s.* New York, NY: Priority Press.

Rossi, P. H. (1990). The old homeless and the new homelessness in historical perspective. *American Psychologist, 45,* 954-959.

Rossi, P. H. (1994a). Telling points and counterpoints: Responses to the commentaries. *American Behavioral Scientist, 37*(3), 443-447.

Rossi, P. H. (1994b). Troubling families: Family homelessness in America. *American Behavioral Scientist, 37,*(3), 342-395.

Rossi, P. H., Wright, J. D., Fisher, G. A., & Willis, G. (1987). The urban homeless: Estimating composition and size. *Science, 235,* 1336-1341.

Rudestam, K. E., & Newton, R. R. (1992). *Surviving your dissertation: A comprehensive guide to content and process.* Newbury Park, CA: Sage.

Salerno, D., Hopper K., & Baxter, E. (1984). *Hardship in the heartland.* New York, NY: Community Service Society of New York.

Sandefur G. D., & Tienda, M. (1988). *Divided opportunities: Minorities, poverty, and social policy.* New York, NY: Plenum.

Schatz, H. (1993). *Homeless: Portraits of Americans in hard times.* San Francisco, CA: Chronicle Books.

Schneider, E. (1990). Senate Judiciary Committee Hearing. Ford Foundation.

Schorr, L. B. (1988). *Within our reach: Breaking the cycle of disadvantage.* New York, NY: Doubleday.

Senate Committee on Labor and Human Resources. (1991). *Child abuse, domestic violence, adoption and family services act of 1991. Report to accompany S 838. Senate committee on labor and human resources. 102nd Congress, 1st session.* (Report No. CG 024 058). Washington, DC: Congress of the United States. (ERIC Document Reproduction Service No. ED 343 043).

Shinn, M., & Gillespie, C. (1994). The roles of housing and poverty in the origins of homelessness. *American Behavioral Scientist, 37*(4), 505-521.

Shinn, M., Knickman, J. R., & Weitzman, B. C. (1991). Social relationships and vulnerability to becoming homeless among poor families. *American Psychologist, 46,* 1180-1187.

Shinn, M., & Weitzman, B. C. (1994). You can't eliminate homelessness without housing. *American Behavioral Scientist, 37*(3), 435-442.

Shinn, M., & Weitzman, B. C. (1996). Homeless families are different. In Jim Baumohl (Ed.) *Homelessness in America.* Washington, DC: National Coalition of the Homeless.

Sidel, R. (1990). *On her own.* New York, NY: Viking Penguin.

Snow, D. A., & Anderson, L. (1993). *Down on their luck.* Berkeley, CA: University of California Press.

Snow, D. A., & Anderson, L. (1987). Identity work among the homeless: The verbal construction and avowal of personal identities. *American Journal of Sociology, 92,* 1336-1371.

Solomon, C., & Jackson-Jobe, P. (1992). *Helping homeless people: Unique challenges & solutions.* Alexandria, VA: American Association for Counseling and Development.

Sosin, M., Piliavin, I., & Westerfelt, H. (1990). Toward a longitudinal analysis of homelessness. *Journal of Social Issues, 46,* 157-174.

Strasser, J. A. (1978, December). Urban transient women. *Journal of Nursing,* 2076-2079.

U.S. Conference of Mayors. (1987). *Status report on homelessness families in America's cities: A 29 city survey.* Washington, DC: Author.

U.S. Conference of Mayors. (1993). *A status report on hunger and homelessness in America's cities: 1993.* Washington, DC: Author.

U.S. Conference of Mayors. (1994). *A status report on hunger and homelessness in America's cities: 1994.* Washington, DC: Author.

U.S. Department of Education. (1993a). *Adults in transition: A report of the fourth year of the adult education for the homeless program.* Washington, DC: Author.

U.S. Department of Education. (1993b). *The national adult education for the homeless program.* Washington, DC: Author.

U.S. Department of Education. (1995). *Learning to Hope: A study of the adult education program for the homeless program.* Washington, DC: Author.

U.S. Department of Housing and Urban Development. (1995, August).*Homeless Assistance Grants Announcement.* Washington, DC: C-Span.

U.S. Department of Labor. (1991). *Job training for the homeless: Report on demonstration's first year.* (Research and Evaluation report Series 91-F). Washington, DC: Employment and Training Administration.

U.S. Department of Labor. (1994). *Employment and training for America's homeless: Report on the job training for the homeless demonstration program.* Washington, DC: Employment and Training Administration.

U.S. General Accounting Office. (1985). *Homelessness: A complex problem and the Federal response.* Washington, DC: Author.

U.S. General Accounting Office. (1988). *Homeless mentally ill: Problems and options in estimating numbers and trends.* Washington, DC: Author.

van Ry, M. (1993). *Homeless families: Causes, effects, and recommendations.* New York, NY: Garland Publishing.

Waxman, L. and Trupin R. (1994). *A status report on hunger and homelessness in America's cities: 1997.* Washington, DC: U.S. Conference of Mayors.

Weiner, L. (1984). Sisters on the road. In E. H. Monkkonen (Ed.), *Walking to work: Tramps in America, 1790-1935.* (pp. 171-188). Lincoln, NE: University of Nebraska Press.

Weir, M. (1992). *Politics and jobs: The boundaries of employment policy in the United States.* Princeton, NJ: Princeton University Press.

Wolch, J., & Dear, M. (1993) *Malign neglect: Homelessness in an American city.* San Francisco, CA: Jossey-Bass.

Wright, J. D. (1988, July/August). The worthy and unworthy homeless. *Society,* 64-69.

Wright, J. D. (1989) *Address unknown: The homeless in America.* New York, NY: Aldine De Gruyter.

Wright, J. D., & Lam, J. (1987). The low-income housing supply and the problem of homelessness. *Social Policy, Spring,* 48-52.

Wright, J. D., & Weber, E. (1987) *Homelessness and Health.* Washington, DC: McGraw-Hill, Inc.

Ziefert, M., & Brown, K. S. (1991). Skill building for effective intervention with homeless families. *Families in Society: The Journal of Contemporary Human Services, 72,* 212-219.

Index

adult literacy, 8

conclusion:
    component importance, 120
    current program description,118
    effective
        demographics/components,
        120, 121
    participants profile, 119
    program components, 119, 120
    program outcome, 120
continuum of care:
    system, 25
    components, 25

economy:
    education, 7- 8
        public, 8
    job training, 7- 8
education:
    basic skills, 8-9, 29, 38
    lack of, 3
    parenting, 8
emergency shelters, 23- 24
Emergency Shelter Grant Program,
    23
employment, 26-30

family shelters, 24, 26, 29

Family Support Act, 128
Federal Emergency Management
    Agency, 23
feminization of poverty, 19
Food Stamp Program, 131-132

General Assistance, 132

Hobbs Stimulus Act of 1983, 23
homeless, families:
    causes, 6
homeless, women:
economic factors, 19-20
    social, 19-20
    structural, 19
    history, 17-19
    18th century, 17
    19th century, 17
    20th century, 17-19
homeless, women with children:
    background, 3, 7
    domestic violence, 7
    family of origin, 3
    foster care, 7
    inadequate healthcare, 7

poor education, 7
substance abuse, 7
causes, 22
housing, 22
psycho social, 22
disadvantaged by, 3
education, 3
ethnicity, 3
income status, 3
earning capacity, 7
economics, 6
poverty, 6
profile, 20-22
age, 21
education, 21
ethnic composition, 21
government program
participation, 21
marital status, 22
number of children, 22
residential status, 22
statistics, 6
social supports, 7
homelessness:
causes, 6, 15-16
housing, 6
personal, 15-17
structural, 15-16
characteristics, 13-16
definition, 11
numbers of homeless, 12-13
patterns of, 11-12
chronic, 12
episodically, 12
temporary, 12
policy, 6
children, 6
education, 6
housing , 6
shelter, 6

Housing Choice and Community
Investment Act of 1994, 25

job readiness, 8, 29
job training: 3, 8-9, 28-29, 30
lack of, 3
programs, 8
job search assistance, 8

life management skills, 8

manpower training programs:
Civilian Conservation Corps, 30-
31
Comprehensive Employment
Training Act of 1973, 133-
134
Job Training Partnership Act,
134-135
Emergency Employment Act of
1971, 133
Job Training Partnership Act, 31-
32
Manpower Development and
Training Act of 1962, 132-
133

National Coalition for the Homeless:
6, 29

parenting skills: 8
program areas and components:
case management, 38
child care, 38-39
client participation, 39
commitment and communication,
39
educational enhancement, 39
employment training and
placement, 40

foster care prevention, 39
health services, 39
independent living skills, 39
needs assessment, 38-39
on-site delivery of services, 39
post placement services, 40
substance abuse treatment, 39
transportation assistance, 38-39

recommendations:
    framework, 121-125
    future research, 125-126
research methods:
    analysis of data, 47- 49
        alpha level, 48
        chi-square, 48
        one-way analysis of variance,
            48- 49
        Scheffe Test, 49
    descriptive survey, 43
    limitations of the study, 49
    population, 44
    problems, 43
    research design, 45, 52
        expert panel, 45- 46
        questionnaire, 45- 47
        pilot test, 46
        response rate, 47
    summary, 50

Social Security Administration, 130-
    131
Social Security, 130
SSI/SSDI, 130-131
Statistical Program for the Social
    Sciences, 47
Stewart B. McKinney Homeless
    Assistance Act of 1987:
    act, 23-24, 29, 32, 33-38, 127
    education, 33

homeless women, 33
job training, 33
programs, 33, 34
    Adult Education for the
        Homeless, 33-35
    Education for Homeless
        Children and Youth, 34
    Family Support Center
        Demonstration Projects, 34
    Homeless Demonstration
        Program, 34
    Job Training for the
        Homeless Demonstration
        Program, 33, 35-38
    Supportive Housing Program,
        34
study:
    goals, 9, 43- 44. See also study
        findings
    purpose, 9, 43
    research questions, 9
    significance, 10
study findings:
    goal 1 (characteristics of
        transitional programs), 51-
        68
    age of children, 61
    age of participants, 59
    educational level, 62
    employability, 66
    employment status, 62-63
    funding sources, 55
    linkages, 55
    marital status, 60
    number and type of
        participants, 59
    number of children, 61
    number of family living units,
        54
    program description, 54

program length, 54
racial status, 59-60
reason for homelessness, 62
respondent locations, 53
goal 2 (current program areas and
    components), 51, 70-93
    adult basic education, 74
    case management, 69
    children's programs, 69
    cultural and recreational
        activities, 74
    educational institutions, 78
    employment training, 74
    employment training
        organizations, 81-82, 86
    family and independent living
        skills, 69
    family health and
        preservation, 69
    follow-up funding levels, 76
    hours in employment
        training, 76
    importance, 86, 91
    length of follow-up services,
        75
    outcomes, 91-92
    permanent housing
        assistance, 69
    support services, 69
    types of case management
        and support services, 74
    types of employment training,
        76
    types of job placement
        services, 78
    where programs components
        are provided
goal 3 (successful program areas
    and components), 52, 93-
    116

demographics, 93, 96-97, 102
program areas and
    components, 102-103, 107
program model, 109-110
summary, 117-118
support services: 8
    child care, 8
    permanent housing placement, 8

The Housing and Community Act of
    1992, 34
The National Commission for
    Employment:
    1990 research findings, 32

Transitional Housing:
    education, 7
    employment, 7
    family structure, 3
    housing, 7
    life skills, 3
    parenting, 3
    policy recommendations, 7
    programs, 23-25
        Supportive Housing
            Demonstration Program,
            24
        Transitional Housing
            Program, 25

U.S. Department of Housing and
    Urban Development, 24
U. S. Conference of Mayors:
    1994 survey, 4, 7, 24, 44,-45
U.S. Department of Health and
    Human Services:
    Aid to Families with Dependent
        Children, 129-130
    Community Services Block
        Grant, 130

Medicaid, 130
Medicare, 130
U.S. Department of Housing and
    Urban Development:
    Community Development Block
        Grants, 23, 128-129
    Operation Bootstrap, 129

Section 8 Rental Certificate
    Programs, 129
Section 8 Voucher Program, 129
U.S. Department of Labor:
    Employment Service, 128
    Unemployment Compensation,
        128

For Product Safety Concerns and Information please contact
our EU representative GPSR@taylorandfrancis.com Taylor & Francis
Verlag GmbH, Kaufingerstraße 24, 80331 München, Germany

T - #0037 - 270225 - C0 - 216/138/12 [14] - CB - 9780815333166 - Gloss Lamination